Frank Sharp

NATIONAL BANKERS LIFE STOCK TRANSACTIONS

July 22 — Mutscher, Shannon, McGinty and Schulte bought NBL stock with loans from Sharpstown State Bank.

July 25

Governor Smith and Doctor Baum bought NBL shares with loans from Sharpstown.

Aug. 4 — Heatly bought NBL shares with Sharpstown loan.

Doctor Baum appointed to State Banking Board.

Mutscher, Shannon, and McGinty sold most of their NBL stock; Schulte sold all of his.

Sept. 11 — Baum and Smith sold most of their NBL stock.

Sept. 12

Heatly sold most of his NBL stock.

Smith and Baum sold the rest of their stock; Baum bought more ... tually, it appeared that the ... Smith and Baum was done ... credited to their account ... purposes on Oct. 6)

Sept. 30

Oct. 6 — Mutscher bought an additio... ... of NBL stock with a $340,000 personal loan

Oct. 8 — from Sharpstown.

TE
UND
CL

TEXAS UNDER A CLOUD

BY
SAM KINCH JR.
AND
BEN PROCTER

JENKINS PUBLISHING CO.
Pemberton Press
Austin and New York
1972

PUBLISHER'S NOTE

The goal of the authors in writing this book, and of myself in publishing it, has not been to deprecate individuals but to point out vitally needed reform. No better way exists to explore the ugly abuse of power, manipulation, and political chicanery in the current Texas political system than to present the history of the stock fraud scandal and those involved in it, followed by explicit recommendations for reform.

That this work is a political hot potato is not denied, and it is our hope that its effect will be felt immediately in the present 1972 elections, by the election of candidates dedicated to reform. That the work is a social documentary of our era that will guide future reform efforts and have an impact and be of interest beyond our own time is, however, our deeper hope and wish. It has certainly been the main goal from the very incipiency of the idea for the book.

The authors are eminently qualified for this task. Sam Kinch, Jr., a brilliant young political analyst, is Capitol columnist for the Dallas *Morning News*. Dr. Ben Procter, one of Texas' leading historians, received his Ph.D. from Harvard and is professor of history at Texas Christian University. In addition to becoming thoroughly familiar with the formidable quantity of public records surrounding the SEC and other investigations, they have recorded hundreds of hours of private interviews with those connected with the case. All facts and quotations presented in this work are backed up by tape-recorded interviews, letters, signed statements, or official public documents.

Like most Texas citizens, I followed the events of the scandal in the newspapers on a day-to-day basis as they unfolded. But the extent of the involvement of our state officials and the breadth and depth of perversion of our legislative system did not hit me with full force until I received the final manuscript of this work. Reading the whole story with all the pieces fitted together for the first time will, I believe, be a shocking experience for any citizen interested in good government for Texas.

Austin   John H. Jenkins
February, 1972

CONTENTS

ILLUSTRATIONS

CHAPTER
ONE

Sorting the Facts

It is difficult to believe, now that the great Texas stock-fraud scandal has been publicized around the world, but when the Securities and Exchange Commission filed its civil suit on January 18, 1971, most Texans did not even know about it.

Many of the state's newspapers did not report the filing of the suit at all in their January 19 editions. Because it happened late on a Monday evening, many radio and television stations failed to report anything about the case until Tuesday afternoon or evening.

In addition, most persons who knew the sketchy outline of the case early did not begin to realize how sweeping the SEC's allegations were until later in the week.

A number of factors impinged on immediate news coverage of the SEC case—some of them relevant to an objective news judgment, some of them not. But the most crucial single factor was the sheer size of the SEC effort. For by the time SEC investigators completed their initial work and the SEC attorneys filed the suit, there were literally hundreds of thousands of words of information.

Predictably, then, it took several days for the ten or twelve reporters who were centrally involved in on-the-spot coverage of the case to get even the gist of it—the enormity of the charges, much less the minute details of the allegedly illegal actions. Similarly, it took the first 48 hours for these same reporters to fight and scratch over enough SEC documents to grasp authoritatively the depth of corruption in Texas government that the SEC was spotlighting. It took still longer, of course, for the nuances of corruption to seep into the minds of the public.

Waggoner Carr, former attorney general and 1966 Democratic candidate for the U.S. Senate, was the only "big name" politician mentioned at first in the case. In the public mind, at least, his career had been over since his defeat in the 1968 Democratic gubernatorial primary. John Osorio, a former aide to Governor Allan Shivers and a former member of the State Board of Insurance, was a big name to long-time watchers of Texas politics, but he certainly had no name-identification with the public.

As newsmen rummaged through the SEC's treasure trove of information, they learned a great deal about this little-publicized federal agency. The SEC is essentially a watchdog, rather than a real law enforcement arm, for the federal government. It has a reputation as a "low caller," more given to understatement than to overstatement and more likely than most federal agencies to avoid political decisions. The SEC's reputation also is such that, relative to other federal agencies, the SEC's court actions often are either unchallenged or contested solely as to the particularity of responsibility.

Newsmen learned all this over a period of time. And perhaps in that same time, the public began to understand how thoroughly the SEC had investigated the stock-fraud case.

But in mid-January, 1971, Texans were not worrying about legal matters or federal agencies' reputations. They were apprehensive, by and large, about the beginning on January 12, 1971, of a legislative session which clearly would have to raise $600 million or more in new and higher taxes. The same legislative session almost certainly would make record-high state government appropriations for the following two-year budget period.

For Texas Republicans, it also was the beginning of a particularly grim moment in history. They had nearly won a second U.S. Senate seat and had come close enough to beating Governor Preston Smith, who had been unopposed in the 1970 Democratic primary, that they could take some comfort. But in the Texas legislature, Republicans could claim only 7 percent of the 181 members. In the wake of President Nixon's defeat by only 39,000 votes in Texas in 1968, the elections of 1970 obviously were a poor showing for the GOP.

For Texas Democrats, on the other hand, it was a banner year—particularly for those of the conventional-wisdom, conservative stripe. They had swept all state-wide offices (dumping, in the process, U.S. Senator Ralph Yarborough, the only liberal holding a major office) and had firm control over the legislature. In mid-January, they were, for the most part, congratulating themselves on the supreme feat—of having alienated liberal Democrats with Yarborough's defeat in the primary, but of having bounced back with a show of unity and having won control of the state government for another two years.

Yet by the time thousands of members of the Democratic establishment gathered in Austin the night of January 18, 1971, for a "victory gala" preceding the state inauguration the next day at noon, the more perceptive among the Democratic leaders knew something was wrong. Some of the later-to-be-revealed principals in the SEC case already had been called in to give depositions about the stock-fraud allegations. But as tightly as that information can be kept secret in some circumstances, total security was impossible in this instance, particularly when so many political futures were potentially at stake. (Many top Texas Democrats, for example, had been trying for months, without any sign of success, to oust state chairman Elmer Baum.)

So the Democratic "gala" mood, like the mood of Texas generally on the night of January 18, was tinged with considerable foreboding. By noon of January 19, the conservative Democratic establishment might as well have held the political version of a wake for its previously victorious forces.

Those cautious men from the SEC had done their homework. They had prepared their stock-fraud suit—a civil proceeding that never could have involved more than a slap on the wrist for anybody—with the precision and timing of genuine professionals. The documents attendant to the suit and the unfolding of the grotesqueries behind the suit were made available and were explained in such a sequence and with such persuasive force that, within a few days, it seemed as though the entire fabric of state government was in danger of suffering irreparable damage.

Indeed, what the SEC alleged in its original civil action paled into a misdemeanor compared to the grosser felony of newly revealed corruption. While the specific acts of alleged wrongdoing are significant in and of themselves, there is a larger and far more venal problem for the people of Texas—the perversion of state government from *public* service to *private* service, the use of public office for private gain, and the stark reality that, unless something is done, the same attitudes and behavior will continue.

Anyone who is familiar with the SEC-initiated revelation of the stock-fraud case must concede that there remains, and probably will remain for years, the conservative Democrats' question of whether the timing of the suit was consciously designed to be politically damaging. There is good evidence, for instance, that Texas banking and insurance officials asked the SEC to delay filing the suit until coordination and cooperation with state agencies could be achieved. These requests were rejected by the SEC—apparently in large measure because those same state officials earlier had known the financial conditions of the banks and insurance companies involved and had taken no definitive action. At the same time, no one has yet given an adequate answer to why the SEC civil suit was filed on January 18—with the news breaking, at least for many Texans, on inauguration day—rather than on, say, January 11 or January 25.

On the other hand, the conservative Democrats' other major complaint—that the SEC suit was "politically inspired"—is specious. If the suit were politically inspired, obviously there would have been no substance to it. And yet the SEC suit, in almost all of its particulars, did not seem politically inspired to Federal District Judge Sarah T. Hughes, a Texas Democrat herself, because she agreed with SEC lawyers on most civil aspects of the case.

It is not the goal of this work, however, to analyze

the whys and wherefores of the SEC action—although certainly that will be worthy of intensive study after all aspects of the stock-fraud case are settled by the courts.

The authors' goals, rather, are to analyze the political impact and significance of the stock-fraud case; to pinpoint where the kind of influence-peddling alleged by the SEC fits into the current pattern of Texas government and politics; and to suggest where the fallout of the stock-fraud controversy should lead in terms of reform. If it is necessary on occasion to extrapolate from the microcosm of the stock-fraud case to the macrocosm of Texas politics, the authors beg the indulgence of the reader. For the cause of good government can best be served by a serious look backward at what *has* happened, an intensive study of what *is* happening, and a vision of what *should* happen in the future.

CHAPTER
TWO

Inaugural Gala

From all across the state people were flocking into Austin on January 18, 1971: newly elected representatives and senators, Democratic officials and party workers, businessmen and prominent local citizens who had contributed to victory—or were being set up for future donations—and excited citizens who were attracted by the spectacle of politics and were impressed with the inauguration of a governor. In other words, a bunch of the boys were preparing to whoop it up with Governor Preston Smith at the expensive Democratic Gala Victory Dinner. They had reason to rejoice, to be gleeful and triumphant. In the previous November they had maimed and butchered Republican Party candidates, allowing only a few to escape slaughter at the polls.

For several months an experienced committee headed by former Lieutenant Governor Ben Ramsey and State Democratic Executive Committee Chairman Elmer Baum had prepared every detail. The Victory Dinner (at $30 a head) featured Richard "Cactus" Pryor, an acerbative, delightfully quick-witted "Roast Master" probably better known as the wide-eyed, ingenuous moderator of the Darrell Royal Show, and entertainer Wayne Newton, whom Governor Smith had handpicked after listening to "Mr. Excitement" sing in Las Vegas. The next day's program was designed to be all things to all men. For the reverent, there would be something called a Prayer Breakfast at 7:30 a.m., with ministers purposely exhibited as representatives of different faiths and ethnic groups. For the traditionalists and those who appreciated pomp and ceremony, there would follow at noon on the Capitol steps the time-honored swearing-in cere-

monies of the governor and lieutenant governor amidst
the booming of cannon, the drawing of sabers, and the
stirring strains of martial music. In the afternoon beau-
tiful girls in cars, expensive floats, smartly disciplined
military units, and a number of marching bands would
follow the honored state dignitaries who were to pro-
ceed slowly in cars along spacious Congress Avenue to
a review stand at 11th Street, thereby delighting the
local citizens and visitors as well as satisfying the
curious. That night, at six inaugural balls, Texans could
take their pick of entertainment ranging from such country and western singers as Faron Young, Ray Price, and
Buck Owens of "Hee Haw" television fame, to nationally known square dance callers, "hard rock" musicians
known as the Gripping Force, and Jeannie C. "Harper
Valley PTA" Riley. The climax of the evening, however,
would be at the Austin Municipal Auditorium, where
state leaders and their wives would parade and strut
before thousands of admirers in the inaugural Grand
March.

Seemingly, all was proceeding well on January 18.
That morning and afternoon the State Democratic Executive Committee (SDEC) had approved, without too
much controversy, the eighteen-year-old vote as well as
an appeal to the United States Supreme Court against
the elimination of party filing fees. Then at 7:00 that
evening the Democratic faithful, 3,000 to 3,500 strong,
prepared to enjoy the gala evening as Cactus Pryor
welcomed them to "the Preston Smith-Ben Barnes
Victory Dinner Part II, brought to them through the
courtesy of Paul Eggers and Company." In fact, Pryor
set the tone for the evening by announcing, "I said it
last time and I'll say it again; this victory dinner honoring Governor Smith is a demonstration of what money, a
slick campaign, and an attractive candidate will accomplish in a political campaign . . . [pause] Not a damn
thing if you're up against a plodder like Preston Smith
[loud laughter and applause]. And I must remember to
include Lieutenant Governor Ben Barnes, but his victory wasn't exactly a surprise. His opponent ran around
about as effectively as the Aggie backfield against
Texas."

17

After ten minutes of good-natured jabs, Pryor gave way to Governor Smith who, by wearing a blue polka-dot bow tie with his tuxedo, still hoped rather pathetically to be distinctive and more colorful. With a prepared text, he continued in the same vein (especially since Pryor was supplying him jokes) by barbing the lieutenant governor effectively. Since Barnes had been delaying the announcement of his future political plans, although repeatedly promising to do so, Smith mocked the lieutenant governor for his indecision. "It is my firm resolve," he asserted, "that in 1972 I will be a candidate for governor, or for re-election, or for a third term, or retire to private life. This is a time for statesmanship and I will not be swayed from this decision."

In turn, Barnes was quick to reply, expressing gratitude for such concern regarding his political future. And "to show my appreciation," he stated in addressing the governor, "I'm going to tell you a long time before I tell John Connally what I'm going to do in '72."

In this way the long evening of speech-making, of introducing all state legislators and their wives, of recognizing party leaders, of rejoicing over their wonderful political fortune, began. But already on that night of January 18 a disturbing story was beginning to circulate, rather hush-hush, among a few in the audience, generating consternation and a troubled air of expectancy. As early as that afternoon in the Capitol, Representative Don Cavness of Austin and several other House members had talked quietly among themselves about a big story that was going to break the next day. Supposedly, "the Feds" were after John Osorio and former Speaker of the House and Attorney General Waggoner Carr, both well-respected by the legislators. So there was immediate concern, according to Cavness, because a "scandal might reflect on the legislature which already had more problems than it was able to solve." At the same time several prominent state leaders had been clued in but were not about to spread the rumor except to close personal friends. For instance, Barnes was walking to his seat at the Victory Dinner when Robert Spellings, his administrative aide, called him aside and stated positively that (from reliable

sources) both Smith and House Speaker Gus Mutscher
would be indicted the next day in Houston and that
"depositions had been taken in a federal investigation
involving the passage of two bills surrounding and concerned with Mr. Frank Sharp who owned the Sharpstown Bank and who was the principal owner of
National Bankers Life Insurance Company." After that,
Barnes reflected, "I had a hard time concentrating . . .
on dinner and the festivities, because I knew that I was
going to be a candidate for higher office in 1972."

Most of the party faithful, however, were oblivious
to such direful events. One enthusiastic observer, sitting
in the midst of some SDEC members, and somewhat
upset that no one had informed her about the rumors,
later commented disgustedly: "They would be the last
to know." To which State Senator Oscar Mauzy of
Dallas added: "And the members of the state senate
were right behind." So, far into the night, most Democrats celebrated, splitting up into smaller groups after
the dinner to continue what they had purposely assembled to do.

At 7:30 the next morning, 350 bleary-eyed people
attended the Prayer Breakfast. And everything still
seemed normal and quiet. But not for long; throughout
the city the rumors were spreading. In the coffee shop
of the Downtowner Motel, Frank Inman, a state UAW
official, hurried over to Lois and Garland Ham of Arlington, also UAW people, quickly asking them if they
knew anything about Smith and Mutscher being involved with the Sharpstown Bank. After that the place
was agog with speculation. About the same time, Frank
Cain, a second-year law student at the University of
Texas and a legislative aide to Senator Max Sherman
of Amarillo, was on his way to class upon hearing the
rumor. "It made a big splash in the law school," he
recalled. "All the students were interested," immediately trying to find out more and speculating on the effects
such a scandal would have on state government. Nor
were they too surprised, he stated, the usual cynical
comment being, "Texas politics is continuing its somewhat infamous reputation." In the Capitol, which is
usually a veritable rumor factory, the story found its

way only into isolated pockets, certain secretaries learning about it during the day while others were completely ignorant of anything happening. In the platform party for the swearing-in ceremonies, however, "everyone was whispering," the wife of a Democratic official remembered. The rotunda was a madhouse, the participants fluctuating between shock and relief. One Democratic leader put it this way: "Would you believe that as many bad investments that I've made, this is one thing I'm not involved in. Thank God! I'm home free."

Throughout Tuesday, January 19, therefore, the stories of indictments, of wrongdoing, of scandal, began to steal the show from the inaugural festivities and to dampen the enthusiasm of the star participants. In the afternoon parade one government leader said he sensed an uneasiness in the crowd, feeling that many of the spectators were smolderingly angry and hostile, so much so that he left the reviewing stand. To a certain extent he was right; for on several occasions at 6th and Congress the *Austin American* reported that "a shouting, cursing, and threatening crowd" tried to disrupt the parade, spitting on Texas A&M band members and hurling fruit and bottles at other performers. By 4 p.m. the Austin police had arrested four persons. Then at the inaugural ball, as the party of sixty-four prominent Texans assembled backstage at the Austin Municipal Auditorium in readiness for the Grand March, one state official turned to several in the official party and sadly, but prophetically, observed: "We are at what is supposed to be a victory and yet what in many ways might also be a funeral. I've been in this business a long, long time, and one piece of advice I'll offer you is that if you want to stay in this business, then always be a pallbearer. All the guys in that category stay alive a long time. But once you start reaching up, and get up, there's nothing to do but get killed off."

Despite maintaining some semblance of happiness and gaiety, the Democratic leaders were getting "up tight" or, in the vernacular of the Capitol, "goosey." Earlier, at the parade, Governor Smith had been unusually quiet and, to some, distant. But that night at the different balls both he and Barnes were definitely cold to each other: during the first inauguration they had attended the several functions together, but now they traveled in separate cars, scarcely acknowledging each other's presence. Hence, the already sizable chasm between the two men was becoming even more unspannable. For that matter, the whole inaugural was a traumatic experience to several first-time participants, a nightmarish memory that they would like to have erasde. Months later, several agreed with the sentiments in a poem written by former Senator Carlos Ashley of Llano:

> O the glamor and the clamor
> That attend the affairs of state
> Seem to fascinate the rabble
> And to some folks seem just great.
> But when the final scale is balanced
> In the field of loss and gain,
> Not one inauguration
> Is worth a good slow two-inch rain.

Through news releases and front-page stories, the stock-fraud scandal was commonplace knowledge by Wednesday morning, and the Capitol was buzzing and reverberating over every new piece of information. In the different offices and at the basement coffee shop, everyone was reading the latest scoop or swapping rumors. "You'd have to get here early in the morning to get a newspaper," a legislative aide recollected. "They were all sold out in a matter of minutes"—and understandably so. By Thursday certain House members were asking Mutscher to step down from the Speaker's Chair and lay out the true situation; rumors concerning the governor and speaker were rampant; and speculation concerning future revelations on other state officials was expected, if not hoped for. In the House, for instance, a number of members wanted relief from the spotlight focused upon them. Or, putting it more graphically, one legislator candidly said: "We hoped that the SEC would catch that red-headed S.O.B. presiding over the Senate."

Yet, as the stories broke each day, revealing to Texans the confusingly intricate manipulation of stocks and the involvement of state officials, the reactions around the Capitol seemed to reflect the state in microcosm. Of course, many people were "sick" and "shocked" over what had happened. "It was like someone hit me in the stomach with a sledgehammer," freshman Representative Gib Lewis of Fort Worth confessed. "Here was my first day in office and I was already declared a crook."

At the same time, some were incensed over the treatment accorded those tainted by the scandal. After all, Smith, Mutscher, *et al.*, were merely "investors," one secretary explained, "and were probably moving a little too fast." If anything, they were victims of a Republican plot, with former Attorney General Will Wilson as the main culprit. From his position in the U.S. Justice Department, she reasoned, "he tried to get back at some of those people who blocked . . . his political career."

About an equal number, however, were delighted over such revelations. "My first reaction was that I was just elated," a legislative aide admitted. "I've worked down here five years and always felt that this thing went on. . . . Now somebody finally got caught at it." Several secretaries wholeheartedly agreed. In their circle of friends "everybody was pretty jubilant," they announced, because "no one liked Preston." Besides, they hoped that such disclosures of wrongdoing and malfeasance in office would force legislators to advocate much-needed reforms in state government.

As might be expected, a few tried to appear as "practical" individuals, cynical of government and calloused to human activities. "I think it's about time to look at things realistically," another legislative aide asserted. "Only a few million dollars at the most are involved in this." In comparison, "the state appropriated seven and a half billion dollars. How the state spends that money in the long run is a lot more important . . . than what happens to four or five million." In other words, he unabashedly reasoned, "people can spend the entire legislative session talking and focusing on something like this rather than dealing with the real problems." Then, to bolster his argument even more, he concluded: "After all, the man on the street does not live by the standards that he expects his politician to live by."

No matter what the varied reactions, one theme was consistent with everyone: Before making a final judgment, they wanted to have more facts, to be better informed. What was Sharpstown all about? What laws, if any, were broken? Should the blame fall upon the persons receiving or giving the loans? And most importantly, how could a government official receive an unsecured loan (no collateral) whereas a private citizen could not? During the future months Texans eagerly sought the answers.

Even under such grim, confused circumstances at the Capitol, by which the foundations of government and faith in state leadership were shaken, the people still maintained their sense of humor. Already a Texas dollar, a huge piece of paper with the Sharpstown Bank on it, began circulating throughout the Capitol complex. And already there was the story about the two Aggies who had tried to rob the (by then defunct) Sharpstown Bank.

CHAPTER
THREE

Not an Ordinary Business Deal

It was a self-described Democratic "gala" mood of January 18 and 19, 1971, then, that was interrupted so dramatically and harshly by the Securities and Exchange Commission's filing of the stock-fraud suit. The "gala" mood did not last long, for over a period of days and weeks, the SEC, in not too subtle language, said many of the very Democratic officials being honored in Austin in mid-January were guilty of using their public positions for private gain—and, consciously or unconsciously, in furtherance of a scheme to defraud the stock-buying public.

It took a while for the SEC's charges to sink into the public consciousness. In the civil suit, filed late in the afternoon of January 18 in Dallas federal court, the federal government's "watchdog" securities agency did not at first play its full hand on the political aspects of the case.

The SEC's original document in the lawsuit did not even name the current political figures who were to be involved later. The suit merely detailed the myriad technical and financial transactions that fell within the SEC's narrow jurisdiction, said the transactions were illegal, and asked Federal Judge Sarah T. Hughes to order the defendants—12 corporations, one so-called "pension" trust, and 15 individuals—not to violate the securities laws any more.*

*The 15 individual defendants were Frank W. Sharp of Houston, John Osorio of Austin, J. Quincy Adams of Dallas, Waggoner Carr of Austin, Joseph P. Novotny of Houston, Tom Max Thomas of Austin, Sam Stock of Houston, Michael F. Ling of Dallas, Donald S. Akins of Dallas, Phillip (sic) I. Proctor of Dallas, Wil-

Initial attention focused, logically, on Waggoner Carr, who was the only big-name politician in the group of individual defendants. Originally from Lubbock, he had been speaker of the Texas House of Representatives for two terms, attorney general of Texas for two terms, the unsuccessful Democratic nominee for the United States Senate (in 1966), and an unsuccessful candidate for the Democratic gubernatorial nomination (in 1968). He left politics deeply in debt and became an Austin-based corporate lawyer. Ironically, at the time of the filing of the SEC suit, Carr also was chairman of House Speaker Gus Mutscher's so-called Committee of 100—a group of not-too-private citizens appointed to recommend improved salaries, better staff and facilities, and higher ethical standards for legislators.

Of the remaining defendants in the case, the only halfway political person was John Osorio of Austin, who in addition to his other financial operations was Carr's law partner. But Osorio's claim to political fame, such as it was, had been in the 1950's and he never gained much identity outside of Austin even then. He had been a top staff aide to Governor Allan Shivers, had accepted Shivers' short-term appointment to the State Board of Insurance, and during the 1960's had run the then-Shivers-owned National Bankers Life Insurance Company. Osorio, son of a Mexican-American restauranteur, stayed on at NBL as president after Shivers sold it.

No one else named in the SEC's suit was even well-known outside of his relatively small, generally local sphere of activity. Frank W. Sharp of Houston probably came as close as anyone to having a statewide reputa-

liam B. Strange, Jr., of Dallas, James Farha of Dallas, David Hoover of Austin, Dallas, and Houston, Audy Byram of Dallas, and H. E. McCain of Dallas.

The pension trust named as a defendant was National Bankers Life Insurance Co. Employees Retirement Plan, known in the SEC law suit as NBL Plan.

The 12 corporate defendants were National Bankers Life Insurance Co., Master Control, Inc., Olympic Life Insurance Co., Nashwood Corp., FLAP, Inc., South Atlantic Co., Sharpstown Realty Co., Oak Forest Realty Co., Oak Forest Investment Co., Sharpstown State Bank, Dallas Bank and Trust Co., and City Bank and Trust Co.

tion, if only because he was responsible for the massive, prosperous, and distinctly middle-class suburban sprawl that he modestly named Sharpstown. Sharp also controlled a number of other companies, but only National Bankers Life was particularly well-known. NBL had a somewhat sleazy history and was on the verge of caving in when former Governor Shivers bought it in 1963. Shivers sold control of the by-then-solvent company to Sharp in 1968 and, as it turned out, significantly and symbolically, Sharp essentially bought NBL with its own money.

The only other genuinely "public" name involved in the stock-fraud case from the start belonged to Michael F. Ling, a Dallas stockbroker whose brother James Ling rocked the business world for a few years with a high-flying superconglomerate called Ling-Temco-Vought.

So there was hardly a sign of a major current political name in the SEC's first document dealing with the stock-fraud allegations. And there was no more than scant, outlined mention of any of the political aspects of the case.

After charging that the stock-fraud case defendants acted in concert to mislead and defraud the public, the SEC merely went on casually to say: "The defendants even attempted to avoid further regulation of the (three defendant) banks by the Federal Deposit Insurance Corporation by attempting to have legislation introduced and passed by the Texas Legislature that would enable state banks to be insured by a state-chartered insurance company, and in furtherance of this proposed legislation caused large sums of money to be loaned to certain legislators, legislative employees, and members of the executive branch and arranged for them to acquire [National Bankers Life] stock through Ling & Co. with the loan proceeds, which [NBL stock] defendants then sold for these persons at a price greater than the amount of the loans."

There was little hint at first, then, that "these persons"—all of them active and important political figures —actually made a quarter of a million dollars in profits from the rigged quick-profit bank loan-stock purchase deals offered by Frank Sharp, his associates, and com-

Dr. Elmer Baum, investment partner of Governor Smith.

panies he controlled.

It did not take long, however, for the news media to start ferreting out the political details of the case affecting the politicians. The newsmen had the help of the SEC and Judge Hughes in doing so, for after the suit was filed literally millions of words and thousands of pages of records from the SEC's investigation were made available to the reporters.

Finally, it became obvious that the politicians involved had not, in fact, merely made independent, open-market decisions in the late summer of 1969 to buy National Bankers Life stock, in the thousands of shares—most of it through Ling & Co.'s brokers and most of it with loans from Sharpstown State Bank—and then to sell the stock back at remarkably close intervals for incredibly similar profit margins.

Leading the noncoincidental list of profit-making politicians was House Speaker Gus Mutscher of Brenham, whose theoretical profit totaled about $105,000 if the so-called "spin-off" stock from NBL is included and if the value of the stock he still held is included.* In the Mutscher view, this profit turned to a loss of more than $200,000 if one considers that the $4,800-a-year legislator later went back and borrowed the money to buy 17,000 more shares of NBL stock, which became worthless when NBL folded. The uncharitable view of that money-losing transaction—also financed by Frank Sharp—is that, the second time around, Mutscher did not have the advantage of being told when to sell his NBL stock.

In fairness to Mutscher, all of the original $105,000 profit from the Sharp-arranged bank loan-stock purchase deal was not the speaker's alone. He shared about $35,000 of the profit with his father, a retired farmer who later worked as a part-time retail clerk in Brenham.

The biggest actual profit may have been made by two long-time investment partners—Preston Smith of Lubbock, Governor of Texas, and Dr. Elmer Baum of

*The profit figures for Mutscher, as well as those that follow for Mutscher's father, Heatly, McGinty, and Shannon, are based on what they would have received if they had sold all of their NBL stock at once. Actually, they sold some and held some—and the stock they held became worthless after the scandal arose.

Rush McGinty and Gus Mutscher.

Austin, an osteopath who at that time was the Smith-selected State Chairman of the Democratic Party. Smith and Baum, investing together as they often did on many business ventures, made a profit of about $125,000—or $62,500 apiece—on the Sharp deal. Baum then came back a short time later and made another $6,000 on his own—because, unlike Mutscher, Baum apparently knew when to sell his stock on the second round. Baum became a Smith-appointed member of the State Banking Board immediately after the initial profit-making bank loan-stock purchase arrangement. But the doctor had to resign that job in the spring of 1971 when it became clear that the State Senate would not confirm him in the position because of his involvement in the stock-fraud controversy. In the fall of 1971, Baum also resigned under fire as State Democratic Chairman.

The other big winners in the Sharp sweepstakes were, in no particular order of importance, Rep. W. S. "Bill" Heatly of Paducah, the irascible chairman of the House Appropriations committee, who made, either solely for himself or for himself and his sons, about $48,471 in theoretical profit; S. Rush McGinty of Spur and Austin, Speaker Mutscher's top political staff man, who made about $45,162 in theoretical profit; Rep. Tommy Shannon of Fort Worth, an insurance man himself as well as Mutscher's right-hand man in the running of the House, who made about $36,520 in theoretical profit; and F. C. "Sonny" Schulte of Brenham, the speaker's long-time confidante and advisor on hometown affairs, who made $17,750 or so in actual profit.

The amounts of the quick profits made by Mutscher, McGinty, and Shannon were not even mentioned when they were indicted jointly by a Travis County grand jury on September 23, 1971, on a charge of conspiracy to accept a bribe. But the grand jury did accept the SEC's version of the relationship between the bank loan-stock purchase deals offered by Sharp and the passage of the two banking bills that Sharp wanted approved by the Second Called Session of the 61st Legislature in September, 1969. Mutscher also was indicted singly on a charge of accepting a bribe. John Osorio, who headed the lobbying of the two bills

Bill Heatly.

Tommy Shannon.

(AP Wirephoto)

31

through the Legislature, was not indicted in connection with the alleged bribery, but he was indicted on the same day on a charge of filing a false statement with the State Board of Insurance.*

Given these facts, it would have taken a large stretch of the SEC's imagination to conclude that all of these political figures—independently of each other—would, with only a few exceptions, buy the same company's stock through the same broker with loans from the same bank and then, within a matter of weeks, sell the stock at the same prices at the same time to the same buyer. And, the SEC noted, the stock was sold to the Jesuit Fathers, a religious order, again with only a few exceptions, at a price about $5 per share above the then-current market price—another indication that the deals were not conducted on the open-market level.

The SEC did not stretch its imagination that much. It said Sharp and his cohorts—all of them defendants in the stock-fraud case—arranged the quick-profit bank loan-stock purchase deals for the politicians "in furtherance of . . . proposed legislation" pending before the Legislature in 1969 about the same time the deals were consummated.

The SEC alleged that the two proposed bank bills, sponsored by Shannon, were designed to relieve the Frank Sharp empire's three banks from federal regulation and permit them to have their deposits insured, instead, by state-chartered nonprofit bank-deposit insurance corporations.

There was some doubt from the start, apparently, and even more doubt in retrospect, about what the two bills would have done. Their sponsor, Shannon, and their chief lobbyist, Osorio, argued that the bills would merely allow newly created state-chartered insurance corporations to insure state bank deposits from the maximum Federal Deposit Insurance Corp. coverage (then $15,000, now $20,000) up to a new Texas-sized maximum of $100,000. Thus, they said, the bills would have allowed state bank-deposit insurance supplemental to, but not in place of, the FDIC insurance, and the

*For more details on passage of the banking bills and on the indictments, see the following chapter.

banks buying the state insurance would not be exempt from federal regulation. Critics of the bills—including the SEC, the late Texas banking commissioner, J. M. Falkner, his successor Robert Stewart, and Texas Bankers Association lobbyist Sam Kimberlin, joined even the chief proponent of the legislation, Frank Sharp himself, in arguing that the bills were designed to get the FDIC off the backs of the state banks in Texas.

Whatever the proposed aim or effect of the bills, it is true that Sharp had personal and business reasons for wanting to get Sharpstown State Bank, the keystone of his empire, out from under the stern regulatory arm of the FDIC.

The FDIC had been criticizing many aspects of Sharp's financial affairs for some time when Sharp and Osorio had the banking bills introduced in the Texas Legislature. The FDIC, like the SEC later, was struck by the self-dealing nature of loans made by and to Sharp-controlled banks and corporations, loans made by Sharp's companies to individuals connected with the empire, and the passing around of both loans and stock within the Sharp circle. Quite a few of the bank loans patently violated federal laws, just as quite a few of the insurance company loans violated state laws. The SEC said, too, that most of the stock transactions were illegal.

In summarizing its case against Sharp, Carr, Osorio, and the others, the SEC charged that they "utilized" the Jesuit Fathers of Houston, Inc.—a trusting but nonprofit group supporting the Strake Jesuit College Preparatory School—as a "conduit" for obtaining about $6 million in funds. The money, said the SEC, was used to manipulate the common stock of National Bankers Life, Olympic Life Insurance Co., and Master Control, Inc., primarily through the services of the Ling & Co. brokerage firm. The SEC said, too, that the funds of the three banks involved—Sharpstown State, City Bank and Trust Co. of Dallas, and Dallas Bank and Trust Co.—were used in the stock manipulation, as well as money extracted from and common stock in NBL, Olympic, Master Control, and RIC International Industries. The SEC also said Ling & Co., with the defendants' guidance

and assistance, caused the supply of NBL, Olympic, and
Master Control stock to be decreased by purchasing it
in the open market—thus driving the price upward arti-
ficially. And the NBL, Olympic, Master Control, and
RIC stock being sold, pledged as collateral for loans, or
otherwise disposed of for value never was "the subject
of any effective registration with the Securities and
Exchange Commission," the SEC charged.

More importantly, perhaps, in light of subsequent
developments, the SEC accused Sharp and the other
defendants of lying, in effect, to both the stock-buying
public and to state and federal regulatory agencies
about the real financial condition of the companies involved and about the ownership and self-dealing nature
of proposed mergers among them.

It was this larger pattern of stock manipulation, de-
ception, and outright fraud that the SEC concentrated
on—at least until the political aspects of the stock-
fraud case began to attract public notice. For as the
SEC said in a February 1, 1971, memorandum in support of its civil law suit, "this situation [the Sharp
business operations] cannot be viewed in the context
of ordinary business practice. The facts establish that
these companies were used as nothing more than a
vehicle for the enrichment of the promoters, with a
complete disregard for any potential harm to the
public."

Federal Judge Sarah Hughes agreed, essentially, with
the SEC. After a twelve-day trial in Dallas, on September 16, 1971, she issued permanent injunctions against
almost all of the defendants.* In an amended judgment
on the SEC's case, dated November 18, 1971, she ruled:
"Throughout the period of the violations [approxi-

*Permanent injunctions were issued after the trial against
Carr, Osorio, Nashwood Corp., Hoover, Adams, Byram, Farha,
Proctor, Sharp, Sharpstown Realty Co., Oak Forest Investment
Co., South Atlantic Co., and Thomas.

The following defendants consented to permanent injunctions,
without admitting the SEC's allegations, either before or during
the trial: Dallas Bank and Trust, City Bank and Trust, Novotny,
Ling, Strange, FLAP, Inc., Stock, Akins, and McCain.

The SEC dismissed, without prejudice, its request for permanent injunctions against the following companies, all of which
are defunct and are in federal or state conservatorship or receiv-

F. C. Schulte, Speaker's aide.

mately June, 1968, to January, 1971], the defendants made numerous securities transactions in which they arranged financing at institutions under their control and used the institutions to bail them out when the transactions became unsupportable. They repeatedly shifted assets of these companies, consolidated and transferred personal loans among the controlled entities, and converted the corporation assets for their personal gain. The transactions established by the evidence are repleat [sic] with self-dealing. Besides the fraudulent acts in dealing with these public companies, certain of the defendants attempted to influence state and federal officials in furtherance of their scheme."

The "influence" of state officials definitely referred to the quick-turnover, quick-profit bank loan-stock purchase deals arranged by Frank Sharp and others for Governor Smith, Dr. Baum, Speaker Mutscher, Representatives Shannon and Heatly, and speaker's aides McGinty and Schulte.

The "influence" of federal *and* state officials also apparently referred to the fact that Sharp made loans to and/or arranged money-making opportunities for two federal banking examiners and at least two state banking examiners, all of whom were supposed to be checking into the operations of Sharpstown State Bank. (The bank examiners were indicted on federal charges in Houston on September 29, 1971.)

Just a week after Judge Hughes' initial ruling on the stock-fraud case, Speaker Mutscher, Representative Shannon, and McGinty were indicted in Austin on charges growing out of the lawsuit that had been filed eight months earlier. The September 23, 1971, indictments came too late, of course, to affect the conduct of the House of Representatives in 1971. But the fact of the indictments forced a great deal more soul-searching among legislators and others about what went on in 1969 and what should be done to prevent its recurrence.

ership: National Bankers Life, NBL Plan, Olympic, Sharpstown State Bank, and Master Control.

Judge Hughes refused to issue an injunction againt Oak Forest Realty Co.—the only instance in which she ruled against the SEC. The SEC did not consider Oak Forest Realty Co. a major offender, however.

CHAPTER FOUR

It All Happened So Fast

Texas humorist and commentator John Henry Faulk summarized most succinctly what many of the state's voters were thinking in 1971 when he said, "Spectacular feats are being performed in the game of Texas politics today. Never in Texas history have so few done so much to so many in the interests of so few."

He referred to the Legislature's September, 1969, passage of the two bills allegedly at the political heart of the stock-fraud case. It was one of those classic cases that lobbyists dream of and the state Capitol press corps warns about—the use of public policy for private gain.

All of the basic elements were there: The poorly paid and understaffed legislators at that special session (the second of the year) were under pressure from their constituents to do their job and go home, if only to avoid spending more state money. They were not, for the most part, informed about even the generalities— much less the specifics—of the two bills they were passing so quickly. Yet a few legislative leaders had been convinced—either by the bank loan-stock purchase deals or by more conventional lobbying—that the proposed legislation was not only worthwhile to the public but also in the special interest of a large and influential segment of the Texas business community, namely, bankers—and, more particularly, the so-called "small" bankers.

The initial major actors in this scenario were central in the latter-day political aspects of the stock-fraud case:

—Governor Preston Smith. He shared a $125,000

quick-turnover stock profit with his investment partner, Dr. Elmer Baum of Austin, then state Democratic Party chairman and immediately afterward a Smith-appointed member of the state banking board. Smith took affirmative action to have the Legislature consider the Frank Sharp-proposed bank-deposit insurance bills. Without Smith's official words expanding the last-minute "call" of the special session—to include "legislation providing for additional insurance on bank deposits"—the two bills never would have been at issue, because they could not have been passed, constitutionally, without Smith's first having said they could be considered by the Legislature. Governor Smith later could not recall who convinced him the two bills should be submitted for special-session consideration, although both Frank Sharp and John Osorio, the Austin lawyer-lobbyist and National Bankers Life Insurance Co. president, said House Speaker Gus Mutscher took credit for so convincing the governor.

—Speaker Gus Mutscher. He made a bundle from the Frank Sharp stock deal bonanza, more than six months after he had first discovered that Sharp wanted the bank-deposit insurance legislation passed and only a couple of months after Mutscher first told Sharp about stock losses that Mutscher had suffered in an earlier deal. Mutscher apparently put out an inordinate amount of effort to get Sharp's bills through the Legislature—not just in the House, but also in the Senate. Mutscher, of course, denied there was anything wrong with the fact that he made money off Sharp's bank loan-stock purchase deal and, about the same time, helped pass Sharp's bank-deposit insurance bills. Sharp, who was granted immunity from prosecution in return for his cooperative testimony, said he and Mutscher had a "tacit understanding" about the relationship of those two events.

—Representative Tommy Shannon of Fort Worth. He made less than Mutscher off the Sharp-arranged unsecured bank loan for purchase of National Bankers Life stock. But Shannon, a successful insurance man himself, took the key front-man role in passage of the two bank-deposit insurance bills. Shannon, even before he

John Osorio.

sponsored the two bills in the August 27, 1969, to September 9, 1969, special session of the Legislature, had obtained House approval for a study of the entire banking system in Texas—with special emphasis on bank-deposit insurance legislation. Then he sponsored the subsequently controversial bills—before the study of the subject was even under way, much less completed —and secured passage of the Frank Sharp bills with the help of Governor Smith, Speaker Mutscher, lawyer-lobbyist John Osorio, and others.

But the bills did not originate with Shannon or Mutscher or Smith. Frank Sharp initiated, publicly at least, the idea of the state-chartered bank-deposit insurance corporations, while he was experiencing problems with the Federal Deposit Insurance Corp. examiners working at his Sharpstown State Bank.

The FDIC examiners were questioning Sharpstown Bank officers about a number of loans—totaling more than $20 million—that the bank had either made to or "bought" from other companies and individuals associated with Frank Sharp. The loans, combined with money that the Securities and Exchange Commission said was "systematically looted" from National Bankers Life and other companies, ultimately were defaulted to such an extent that Sharp's entire financial superstructure decayed and collapsed. The FDIC examiners also questioned other Sharpstown Bank practices, but the self-dealing and generally undercollateralized loans absorbed most of the federal officials' attention.

One of the FDIC examiners, however, had more than a mere adversary-style professional interest in Sharp's affairs. Ted Bristol, who later was indicted for accepting financial favors from Sharp, received from Sharp a gift of 700 shares of National Bankers Life stock. The shares were bought in his wife's name through the brokerage account of Will Wilson, who was then Sharp's top legal advisor.*

*Wilson joined the Nixon Administration in 1969 as the nation's top criminal law enforcement officer. He resigned in the fall of 1971 after criticism of his business and professional ties to Sharp became too acute. Bristol left the FDIC in early 1971 to become president of the Sharp-owned City Bank and Trust Co. of Dallas. He resigned that position in late summer of 1971.

According to Sharp, Bristol originally suggested the possibility of the state's creating its own bank-deposit insurance system for state banks. Sharp said the proposal was designed, from the beginning, to "get the FDIC off my tail . . . off my back." And it was Sharp himself, after all, who carried through with actual efforts to establish the deposit-insurance scheme.

Sharp started with House Speaker Gus Mutscher, with whom Sharp had shared a long but somewhat casual and interrupted relationship. He explained to Mutscher in the fall of 1968 what he had in mind about the bank-deposit insurance proposal, couching it in terms of helping small state banks attract larger deposits. The FDIC insured accounts in member banks up to only $15,000 at the time; Sharp wanted the state-chartered deposit insurance to cover accounts up to $100,000. Sharp argued that the smaller state banks frequently had difficulty attracting deposits over the FDIC limit, while the larger banks—particularly the national banks—did not have the same problem because their sheer size constitutes an implied guarantee.

Mutscher seemed impressed with the idea, although he warned Sharp that the Legislature in 1969 faced a long and complicated session over more critical issues. The subject was dropped for the time being, and the only action taken during the regular session of the Legislature in the spring of 1969 was House passage of Shannon's resolution creating a between-sessions study committee to investigate, among other things, the possibility of state bank-deposit insurance legislation.

Sharp did not give up the fight, however. Indeed, as his behind-the-scenes struggle with the FDIC examiners grew more intense in the spring and summer of 1969, he became even more anxious to, as he put it, "get the FDIC off my tail."

At a meeting with Mutscher in the speaker's suite at the Rice Hotel in Houston in July 1969, Sharp brought up the bank-deposit insurance proposal again. Mutscher discussed it briefly and then moved quickly to a subject dear to his pocketbook—his own losses in the stock of Siboney Corp., a company that Sharp once intended to merge with his Sharpstown Realty Co. but never did.

Sharp suggested that Mutscher's loss could be recovered if the speaker would invest in National Bankers Life. Osorio at the time publicly said, as president of NBL that he was planning a program of mergers and acquisitions to make NBL, a billion-dollar corporation. Most of the mergers and acquisitions never took place, and others involved companies already associated with Sharp's conglomerate complex. (The SEC said in its civil law suit in Dallas federal court that the NBL-announced program was part of the scheme to manipulate stock prices.)

After that meeting—which Sharp said ended with a wink, a smile, and a "tacit understanding"—things began to roll right for Sharp. The veteran con man said Mutscher "had a problem [the earlier stock losses] and we were trying to work together. My problem was that I would like for the legislation to be passed."

Working together, in this case, was profitable for Mutscher and his close friends Tommy Shannon, Rush McGinty, and Sonny Schulte. (The four often made investments together or simultaneously.) Within a few weeks, along with Representative W. S. "Bill" Heatly of Paducah, they had borrowed nearly $400,000 from Sharp's bank to buy about 30,000 shares of National Bankers Life stock. Within six weeks of the loan-purchase transactions, the four men sold most of their shares for a combined profit of $198,500.*

The two House members, the speaker, and the speaker's aides were not the only state officials or quasi-officials benefiting from Sharp's generosity. Dr. Elmer Baum, the state Democratic Party chairman at the time, was a neighbor of NBL president John Osorio, as well as an occasional social companion. They talked about business at a meeting in Dallas—again, coincidentally, in late July, 1969—and Baum suggested that he and his investment partner, who just happened to be the Gover-

*Heatly's involvement in the stock deal is obscure, the more so because the chairman of the House appropriations committee has refused to discuss the matter. Superficially, at least, Heatly played no part in the passage of the bank-deposit insurance bills, but his operational technique involves staying in the background, anyway.

Waggoner Carr.

Speaker Gus Mutscher and Lt. Gov. Ben Barnes.

nor of Texas, Preston Smith, might be interested in buying some National Bankers Life stock—*if it could be financed,* Baum said. Within a few days, Smith said later, he went to Dr. Baum's office for a blood shot (Baum, as osteopath, also is Smith's personal doctor). While there, Smith signed a loan application for a business deal which, after Baum explained it, Smith thought "sounded all right." So Baum and Smith borrowed about $275,000 from the Sharpstown State Bank—a bank they had not borrowed from before—and bought 20,000 shares of NBL stock with the loan proceeds. They later sold the stock at about the same time and at approximately the same price as the Mutscher group, netting Baum and Smith a profit of $125,000.

After the loans were made, though, and before the profits were made, strange things began to occur in and around the Legislature.

Frank Sharp, for obvious reasons, had rekindled his enthusiasm for the bank-deposit insurance legislation. He first turned to his right-hand man at the insurance company, NBL president and former state insurance commissioner John Osorio, for advice about the legislative approach to the deposit insurance. Osorio had one of his law partners, Eugene Palmer of Austin, draw up the proposed legislation because Palmer, like Osorio, was an experienced lawyer-lobbyist who had a reputation as a skilled draftsman of lobby-backed legislation. (Palmer was to complain two years later that he never was paid for his work on the bills.) For further assistance in lobbying the bills through the legislature, Osorio enlisted the aid of another law partner, Waggoner Carr of Austin, former speaker of the Texas House and former attorney general of Texas who also was a business partner of Osorio and Sharp.*

It did not take long for Sharp to begin getting results. On August 11, 1969, during the first special session of the Legislature, the House, without debate and with-

*Just before Christmas, 1971, Carr filed a general damage suit in Austin against Sharp, seeking $100 million in personal damages because, Carr said, Sharp either deceitfully and fraudulently or negligently failed to tell Carr about Sharp's stock-fraud and alleged bribery schemes.

out the knowledge of most members, passed a resolution praising Frank W. Sharp of Houston. It was timed to coincide with Sharp's departure two days later for Rome, where he was named a "founder" of the four-centuries-old Society of Jesus for his generosity to the Strake Jesuit College Preparatory School in Houston and where Sharp also was granted an audience with Pope Paul. The author of the resolution was Speaker Gus Mutscher of Brenham.

But the resolution was only the warm-up, because the very next day—August 12—Representative Shannon introduced Frank Sharp's bank-deposit insurance bills, which John Osorio's law partner Gene Palmer had just completed. Sharp had to remain patient, however, for no action was taken on the bills immediately since they were not on the list of subjects that Governor Smith said the Legislature could consider at that first special session. The two bills died in the House banking committee.

A reprieve was granted, though. The Legislature had not completed its business at the first special session—most importantly, it still had to pass a tax bill—so Governor Smith called a second special session to begin August 27. On September 5, Representative Shannon reintroduced the Frank Sharp bank-deposit insurance bills in the House—only five weeks after Shannon and the others had received loans from Sharp's bank to buy stock in Sharp's insurance company.

Under the constitution, the bills technically could not be passed by the Legislature without the governor's having submitted at least the general subject matter as an additional item in the "call" of the special session—or, as often happens, without a constitutional point of order being raised that the legislation had not been submitted by the governor. But it is common practice for legislators to propose bills without the governor's advance approval, in hopes of later getting his consent for legislative action. Smith's submission of "legislation providing for additional insurance on bank deposits" came on September 8, 1969—only three days after Shannon introduced the bills. Smith's memory in early 1972 was perceptive enough to remember that he did not submit the *specific* bills introduced by Shannon, but he could not remember who convinced him that even the subject matter of the bills should be considered in the last minutes of the special session.

The bills were approved by the Legislature with a speed that may be amazing to private citizens who often see the lawmakers take literally months *not* to pass bills. But the fact that the bills were passed and sent to the governor for signature within 48 hours of the time Smith said they could be considered was not uncharacteristic of the whole Frank Sharp scheme.

Representative Shannon had the House banking committee's approval of the bank-deposit bills by noon of September 8. Shannon gave the committee a hasty and superficial explanation of the bills at a brief and lightly attended public hearing, which had been called on short notice. Shannon did not call as witnesses on the legislation any of the state officials who dealt with banking or insurance; nor did he call as witnesses any members of the private banking industry. Banking committee chairman Neal Solomon of Mount Vernon did not demand further testimony. As a result, the bills were only questioned seriously by two members of the banking committee—Representatives Felix McDonald of Edinburg, a crusty veteran curmudgeon, and Charles Patterson of Taylor, a freshman conservative who thought the rush-job procedure was slouchy.

There was little House debate on the bank-deposit insurance bills, because—as usually happens when a bill is hurried through the Legislature—the lawmakers voted on the author's explanation of the bill rather than on the substance of the bill itself. When this procedure is extraordinarily speedy, as it was in the case of the Frank Sharp bills, most members do not have time to study the bill or amendments to it—and often as not, they do not even have copies of the bill and the amendments. For that reason—and because Shannon touted the Sharp bills as being in the interest of the "little banks," which is a great appeal to rural legislators—no more than twelve negative votes were cast against the

Sharp bills in the House.* And the only amendment to the Sharp bills, which was adopted on a motion by Representatives Dave Finney of Fort Worth and Vernon Stewart of Wichita Falls, would have allowed savings and loan associations to purchase the deposit insurance, too.

Within a few hours of the time Governor Smith allowed Frank Sharp's bills to be considered, then, they had been passed by the House and were on their way to the Senate.

In the Senate, however, the pathway to passage had not been strewn with bank-loan and quick-profit stock-purchase deals. The ponderous Senate took more than twenty-four hours to pass the two bills that would have revolutionized the banking industry in Texas and the concept of bank deposit protection in the nation.

Because of oddities in Senate rules of procedure, it was not feasible, so late in the special session, for the Frank Sharp bills to be taken up by the Senate banking committee, which normally would have used its expertise on major bank-related legislation of that type. The slow-moving banking committee would have had to hold public hearings on the bills, because that committee did not have the authority to "floor-report" legislation—that is, give committee approval without benefit of a hearing by simply holding a committee meeting on the Senate floor. Instead, Lieutenant Governor Ben Barnes sent the bills to the Senate's committee on county, district, and urban affairs, the chairman of which was Senator Ralph Hall of Rockwall, and that committee approved the bills almost immediately on the morning of September 9, 1969.

There was a temporary political snafu that threatened to break Frank Sharp's golden egg. Senator Jack Strong of Longview had been designated by Osorio as the Senate sponsor of the Frank Sharp bills. (Strong, who was a bank director, also had been a regional Waggoner Carr campaign manager in the 1966 U.S. Senate race.)

*A maximum of fourteen negative votes was cast on the procedural question of suspending a valuable but commonly ignored constitutional rule requiring that bills be read on three separate calendar days.

But Senator Bill Patman of Ganado "tagged" the bills—preventing their immediate passage—because of a personal feud with Strong and because, Patman said, he had reservations about the wisdom of the bills. Patman withdrew his opposition and removed his "tag," the senator said, after Speaker Mutscher and others convinced him the bills were offered in "good faith" and also after Strong was replaced as sponsor of the bills. Senator Charles Wilson of Lufkin, who was chairman of the Senate banking committee, actually moved the bills through the Senate. (Neither Strong nor Wilson was accused of any wrongdoing in connection with passage of the bills.)

As in the House, there was almost no debate about the Frank Sharp bills in the Senate. Wilson and other supporters explained the legislation as being designed to provide depositors in state banks with account protection above the FDIC's limit and up to $100,000, but not in place of the FDIC's insurance up to the then-maximum amount of $15,000. Wilson and others also said, as had their House counterparts, that there was no opposition to the bills—as, indeed, there was not, since neither state banking and insurance officials nor the private banking community had been consulted by the Legislature.

Only one substantive amendment was adopted in the Senate—an amendment by Senator A. R. "Babe" Schwartz of Galveston to allow private or unincorporated banks to purchase the bank-deposit insurance, too. (Schwartz is a lawyer for Shearn Moody, Jr., who controls the largest private bank in Texas.) Only one negative vote was cast against the bills—by Senator Chet Brooks of Pasadena.

The role of Lieutenant Governor Barnes in the passage of the Frank Sharp bills is not entirely clear, although as presiding officer in the waning hours of a legislative session he certainly had the red light-green light power.

Barnes has stressed that he did not buy National Bankers Life stock, did not borrow money from Sharpstown State Bank, and had no other business dealings with Frank Sharp. He also said he had not pressured senators to vote for the bank-deposit insurance bills, adding that he was not even familiar with the legislation in detail. Senator Strong, the original Senate sponsor of the bills, confirmed that in an August, 1971, affidavit. Strong swore that when he approached Barnes about getting help to pass the bills, "I received the distinct impression he [Barnes] had never heard of them before." Barnes also emphasized that he was not presiding when the bills were passed, though that is an insignificant factor; the presiding officer customarily tells his substitute how he wants specific pieces of legislation handled, anyway.

John Osorio, who lobbied the bills, and Frank Sharp, who originated them, tell entirely conflicting—and not particularly flattering stories—about Barnes' role.

According to Sharp, Osorio reported back to Sharp that Barnes "delivered as he said" on Senate passage of the bills; that Barnes "takes only cash," and that Barnes had been "taken care of" in connection with the bills, so that Sharp was not "indebted" to Barnes.

On the other hand, Osorio said he never told Sharp, nor even suggested, that Barnes had been bribed to get the bills through the Senate. Osorio said only that Barnes provided "procedural help," at Osorio's request, and that the bills "wouldn't have passed without his [Barnes'] help—very simple"—which would have been true about any bill. Osorio also said that Sharp's version of their conversation was "a damned lie."

Whether or not Barnes was "improperly influenced," as the quaint Texas bribery statute says, on September 9, 1969, the Sharpstown Bank bills were passed by the Senate, sent briefly back to the House for concurrence in the Schwartz amendment, and passed on to the governor for his seemingly-certain signature.

At that stage, however, the bank-deposit insurance legislation entered a new period of retrospective mystery. For on September 29, 1969, on the last day he could veto the bills without allowing them to become law with or without his signature, Governor Smith did, in fact, veto them.

Smith vetoed the bills in characteristically unstraightforward language. In the only clear-cut, categorical, and nonsubjunctive part of the veto message, Smith said, "I feel that there is no emergency need for this legislation at this time and that these bills should be vetoed to provide time for a full and complete study (by the Finance Commission) of possible solutions to be considered by a future session of the legislature."

The governor said the bank-deposit insurance legislation was not the proper approach and asserted, without elaboration, that a similar deposit insurance program that operated in Texas for twenty-two years, just after the turn of the century, was "unsatisfactory." He noted there was to be no limit on the number of state-chartered, private nonprofit corporations that would offer the deposit insurance, which Smith said "could lead to a number of small weak private corporations which could not provide the protection anticipated." He also said he feared the bill might be "discriminatory" in that (1) banks with less than $200,000 in capital would only have deposits insured up to one-half of the banks' capital; (2) there might be state banks that were not members of the Federal Reserve System that might cancel their FDIC memberships and thus be relieved of limits on savings account and other interest, to which limits national banks still would be subject; and (3) the same discrimination could arise as between state-chartered and federal savings and loan associations.

Most of the governor's message paralleled precisely arguments against the bills presented—*after their passage*—by the banking industry and its state-agency branch office, the Finance Commission. The commission, entirely controlled by the bankers and their spokesmen, voted unanimously on September 13, 1969, to recommend a veto of the bank-deposit insurance bills. In addition, Governor Smith was urged to veto the bills by the then-president of the Texas Bankers Association, Derrell Henry of Odessa, and by former Governor Allan Shivers of Austin, who is a so-called "big" banker and also a friend of and sometimes adviser to Smith.

But apart from the bankers' outcries, Smith tossed a couple of time-bombs into his veto message, too—ones that did not really explode until sixteen months later when the Securities and Exchange Commission filed its stock-fraud case in Dallas.

In the context of talking about "possible discrimination" between state and national banks and between state and federal savings and loan associations, Smith added: "There is great concern as to the ultimate effects of the withdrawal from federal supervision of banks and savings and loan associations operating under state charters." Again, Smith did not go into any detail. Nor did he elaborate on another phrase used in the veto message—"there has not been opportunity for full public hearings on these bills or on this particular approach to this problem."

Thus, as he had done many times in his political life, Smith walked through the barnyard without messing up his boots. He had made a pile of money off Frank Sharp's bank loan-stock purchase deal. He had initiated the affirmative action to allow the Legislature to consider Sharp's bills. And yet he vetoed Sharp's bills—after, it must be stressed, the banking industry intervened—and in the process, at least by hindsight, took himself off the list of possible bribery suspects, while asking for more detailed investigation of Sharp's proposal.*

*It is instructive, in the aftermath of the stock-fraud case, that nothing further was done to carry out Smith's directive that a study of bank-deposit insurance by state-chartered corporations be made. Representative Shannon's House committee study was activated, but it never produced any recommendations. Representative Fred Orr of De Soto, who has business interests in both banking and insurance, prepared a Frank Sharp-style bank-deposit insurance bill for introduction in the 1971 legislative session, but he dropped the project after the stock-fraud case broke. And the Finance Commission, which was ordered by the governor to study deposit insurance legislation, had done nothing more than budget $6,000 for that purpose. In late 1971, however, the commission showed signs that it would conduct an inquiry and, presumably, have recommendations ready in time for the 1973 session of the legislature.

CHAPTER
FIVE

Preston Smith

"Let him who is without stock throw the first rock," said Preston Smith, governor of Texas, as he began a remarkably clever and self-serving but also self-deprecatory address to the February 6, 1971, Headliners Club stag luncheon in Austin.

It was pure Preston, and perhaps his finest speechmaking performance as governor. There were the typical mispronunciations, bad grammar, inept timing, and poor accenting of words and syllables. As usual, too, Smith had difficulty restraining himself in response to his audience, often swallowing the ends of his jokes before the listeners understood where he was aiming and frequently starting new ones before laughter had died down from the previous cracks.

But the speech, probably the most humorous ever written for or delivered by the governor, achieved its dual purpose: to demonstrate that Smith had maintained his composure during the acute political crisis surrounding the initial weeks of the stock-fraud scandal and to disarm, however temporarily, those critics who had carped on Smith's seeming unwillingness to admit that the crisis existed.

And, lest there be any mistake in historical perspective, in early February, 1971, the entire tone of Texas politics was one of crisis.

The governor, his investment partner and state Democratic chairman Dr. Elmer Baum, House Speaker Gus Mutscher, two of Mutscher's top aides, and two of the most influential House members stood accused, at the very least, of grossly improper ethical behavior. Already there were demands by both private citizens and incumbent office-holders for the resignation or removal from office of those involved in the Securities and Exchange Commission's allegations. Already there were demands, again by both public and private people, for full-scale and wide-ranging investigations of the stock-fraud case.

Most close observers believed that the initial revelations about the involvement of top Texas political personages in the stock-fraud scandal represented only the tip of the proverbial iceberg.

Not so with predictably unpredictable Preston Smith.

At no time did he want to talk about the role of others in the quick-profit bank loan-stock purchase deals arranged by Frank Sharp and his cohorts. From a personal viewpoint, all Smith saw was "a straight business deal" that he thought offered some hope of profit— a deal that he said was handled by Dr. Baum, with whom Smith had been investing for several years. Smith said if the National Bankers Life stock investment had been profitable—by then he knew he and Baum had split $125,000 in profits—it would be one of the few money-making deals they had made. (In addition to securities, they put their money in a variety of other "opportunities," as the governor called them, including a ranch in the hill country northwest of Austin.)

Smith saw nothing wrong with taking the loan from Sharpstown State Bank and buying stock in National Bankers Life, because he said he did not know anything about Frank Sharp's interest in two bank-deposit insurance bills—bills that Smith, after sharing the loan to buy the stock, submitted to the Legislature for emergency consideration, bills that the governor later vetoed after he and Baum had made their profit from Sharp's insurance company stock. There was, to be sure, conflicting testimony as to whether Smith *did* know about Sharp's interest in the legislation. Both Dr. Baum and John Osorio, who lobbied the bills through the legislature, testified separately that Smith was indeed aware of Sharp's interest in the bills.

On the other hand, it was not at all unusual for Preston Smith to see things differently from most of his fellow human beings. For despite one of his favorite self-descriptions—"we're just common folks"—he was, in truth, anything but a common man.

Smith's consistent use of the royal "we" to discuss his thoughts and activities was but one minor indication of his uncommonness. Perhaps, however, he was merely trying to incorporate all of the "just common folks" into his being and thereby elevate their status to his own by use of a collective pronoun.

Preston Earnest Smith had been an unusual fellow all of his life, probably because most of the time he was fighting the odds, doing it his own way, and, most of the time, winning.

Smith's background certainly did not guarantee success of any kind. Born on March 8, 1912, he was the seventh of thirteen children in a hard-working but poor tenant farming family. They left the now-disappearing Corn Hill community in Williamson County in the mid-1920's for the more hopeful dryland farming country of Dawson county, where the Smiths settled on a half-section tenant farm. Smith was not overly-educated during nine years in the rural schools of the times, but he did learn to read. He later recalled when talking about his nearly lifelong desire to run the state of Texas, "I remember when I was nine years old, walking down a cotton row behind a span of mules and reading an old newspaper about Governor Jim Ferguson. That was the first time I had read about a governor and I decided right then and there that I wanted to be governor."[*]

A man did not make it to the top, even in those days, by looking over the rumps of plow-pulling mules, so in his late 'teens Smith left his family farm—on his own —and moved to Lamesa, seventeen miles away. He worked his way through high school, just as he later did in college—at a filling station and whatever odd jobs were available in those trying dustbowl-and-depression days.

By the time he was graduated with a business degree from Texas Tech in 1934, Smith was on his way to

[*]In 1917, Ferguson was impeached and removed from office— on a variety of charges involving abuse of the governor's powers —when Preston Smith was five years old, but Ferguson remained politically active for many years.

prosperity—typically for small businessmen, on borrowed money—in the service station business. (He had operated a leased service station to pay for his college expenses.) He waited nearly a year before marrying a pretty classmate, Miss Ima Smith, and then branched out into the theater business. His first theater, in an abandoned laundry building across the street from the Texas Tech campus in Lubbock, was successful enough to be followed in later years by expansion into a chain of other theaters, including early-day drive-ins. Smith also dabbled in real estate, although he subsequently claimed that a close friend and business associate was simply using Smith's name on a real estate firm in Lubbock. By the time he entered his second term as governor, Smith estimated his financial net worth at $200,000 (based on what he *paid* for his holdings).*

Smith started his lengthy career in politics in 1944 when, at the age of 32, he won the first of three terms in the Texas House of Representatives, a job in which he apparently served with more anonymity than anything else. He then lost two races—in 1950 for lieutenant governor, when he finished a distant third in a field of twelve, and in 1952 for the state senate, when veteran incumbent Senator Kilmer Corbin of Lamesa won narrowly. He ran for the senate again and beat Corbin in 1956.

As a senator for six years, Smith was known among his colleagues as a serious, if not overly-active legislator, more inclined to concentrate his attention on affairs back home than to spend an inordinate amount of time on the study and solution of overall state problems. His philosophical orientation, of course, was conservative and his perspective on the role of government in modern society was strictly that of the plains Democrat. Perhaps because he was not by nature a socializer of the back-slapping, drinking-party variety, Smith was considered by some of his Senate colleagues to be withdrawn and, at times, even autistic.

It was a surprise, then, to many Capitol observers

*When one newsman reported in early 1971 that Smith's financial statement showed a net worth of just under $1 million, the governor did not deny the accuracy of the figure.

Alton Curry, Gov. Preston Smith, and Bob Bullock arriving at the Federal Courthouse in a pickup truck for Smith to give a deposition to the SEC.

that Preston Smith ran for lieutenant governor in 1962 to succeed Ben Ramsey, who had defeated Smith, among others, for the job in 1950 and had been elected to an unprecedented six terms as presiding officer of the Senate. Ramsey was appointed to the Railroad Commission in 1961 by Governor Price Daniel. The lieutenant governor's position remained vacant because Texas law does not provide a means of filling it, although the president pro tempore of the Senate becomes the presiding officer during legislative sessions.

Once more, Smith appeared to be taking the gamble that, the odds-makers were saying, would end his political career. His chief opponent was House Speaker James A. Turman, then considered the liberals' brightest hope for future office-holding, a man younger and more articulate than Smith and also an orator of far greater capacity. The other candidates included three of Smith's colleagues in the Senate—Senators Robert Baker of Houston, Crawford Martin of Hillsboro, and Jarrard Secrest of Temple—all of them experienced and all of them expected to run ahead of Smith.

Predictably, Smith and the others split the conservative vote in the 1962 Democratic primary, thus allowing Turman to take a 69,000-vote margin into the runoff. Unpredictably, however, Preston Smith ran second behind Turman—and then, with the aid of a mini-scandal involving Turman's expense account, Smith surprised many political analysts by coming from behind to win the runoff by more than 50,000 votes.

Smith remained irritated that many of his enemies credited his victory in that 1962 campaign to Governor John Connally, who clearly was a more glamorous candidate in his first attempt to win elective office. Connally won a bitter Democratic primary runoff election against Houston attorney Don Yarborough, another liberal, at the same time Smith was defeating the liberal Turman. The anti-Smith analysis was that the Connally sex appeal, plus the threat of a Yarborough governorship, produced the heavy conservative vote that rejected both Yarborough and Turman. Actually, Smith noted, Connally's margin over Yarborough was a mere 26,250 votes.

It can be argued that Smith's well-publicized personal antagonism toward Connally—which was reciprocated, though with less intensity, by Connally—dated from the postelection analysis of the 1962 races, particularly by members of the Capitol press corps. While Connally constantly courted the press during his six years as governor—with mixed but generally good success— Smith during that same period as lieutenant governor seemed to develop both a distrust of and a dislike for the newspaper reporters who regularly covered state government and, in election years, wrote in detail about political campaigns.

Smith never attempted to conceal his attitudes toward the Capitol press or toward Connally, which may explain why his most dramatic political move was taken at a time when both the reporters and the incumbent three-term governor were other-directed. On August 23, 1967, while reporters were busy speculating that Connally would seek a fourth term, and while Connally was on a six-week safari to Africa sponsored by a television network, Preston Smith—who was then acting governor in Connally's absence—announced that he would run for governor in 1968 regardless of whether Connally sought another term.

Connally did not run again, and Smith once more finished second in a ten-man Democratic primary field —trailing liberal Don Yarborough by more than 35,000 votes. He defeated Yarborough in the runoff by 150,000 votes, or more than five times Connally's victory margin over the same Yarborough six years before. Smith then defeated Republican candidate Paul Eggers by more than 400,000 votes in the presidential-vote heavy general election. Although Smith did not exactly cover himself with glory during his first term in office, in 1970 he became the first Democratic governor in Texas history to be unopposed in the primary*—and again defeated Eggers in the general election, this time by only 158,000 votes.

Despite the fact that he received a total of more than 12 million votes in his statewide races through 1970,

*Smith would have been opposed in the primary by Senator Ralph Hall of Rockwall, also a conservative, but the Texas

Preston Smith continued to confuse, if not also to dismay, the people of Texas. For instance, while the stock-fraud scandal and his name-involvement in it were still on the public's mind, the governor announced on November 20, 1971, that he would seek a third term.* He even said he hoped the passage of the two bank-deposit insurance bills behind the scandal would become a major issue in the campaign because, he emphasized, as governor he had vetoed the bills and thus prevented their enactment into law. He said, too, that the voters should consider him "a hero" because of that veto. He added, in one of the year's most disingenuous political statements, "I don't think there is anything we have done to make people doubt our honesty."

Smith's curious kind of political inconsistency was his trademark. For example, during the 1969 legislative session—when a burgeoning demand for state services appeared to require both a record-high appropriations bill and a sizable tax bill—he took the knee-jerk position that the constitution provided only for a two-year state budget and not for the alternative one-year budget. (Governor Connally had forced a one-year budget through the Legislature over Lieutenant Governor Smith's objection, perhaps increasing Smith's rapture with the constitution.) On June 20, 1969, then, Smith vetoed a one-year budget passed by the Legislature, at Lieutenant Governor Ben Barnes' insistence—a budget that would not have required a tax bill. The veto was accompanied by a derisive Smith comment that the Legislature's "ride-now, pay-later" approach was both

Supreme Court ruled that Hall was constitutionally ineligible because he was a member of the previous Legislature that had voted to raise the governor's salary.

*Smith earlier had been critical of governors, particularly Connally, who sought more than the traditional two two-year terms. When he was assured of winning his second term, Smith told newsmen on election night, 1970, that he might seek a third term. Reminded of his previous opposition to three-term governors, Smith said, "Yes, but that was before I was governor. I have about decided it takes longer than four years to get your program completed." When he formally announced as a candidate for his third term, Smith referred to "the three-term tradition"—a tradition established only by three previous governors: John Connally, Price Daniel, and Allan Shivers.

unconstitutional and un-Texan. Smith's veto left the legislators no choice but to write a two-year state spending plan, and they—not the governor—had to bear the cross of passing a $349 million tax bill.

Yet almost exactly two years later, when the Legislature in 1971 had approved another record-high two-year appropriations bill—and, oddly enough, the taxes to pay for it—Preston Smith, the archconstitutionalist, vetoed the entire second year of the state budget because of uncertainty about the fiscal situation in 1972. This second veto pushed members of the Legislature into the politically awkward position of having to vote for a tax bill in an election year, something politicians generally accept as Number 1 on the "don't" list.

It seemed that Smith's tax-related dealings with the Legislature were hostile, by design. Hardly anything ever worked out right for anyone. In 1969, Smith proposed a complex tax package to the Legislature and warned that the alternative was a corporate income tax, yet he did nothing to encourage adoption of his plan. The lawmakers blithely ignored the governor's proposals, for the most part, and still avoided the tax that is symbolically intolerable to the Texas business establishment. In 1971, Smith earned the nickname "Magic Wand Preston" when he sought the Legislature's—and ultimately the taxpayers'—approval of a series of state-backed bonds which, without an increase in current taxes, would pay for some capital expenditures but which also would pay some of the state's operating expenses, at an enormous long-range cost to the taxpayers. With "ride-now, pay-later" Preston again sitting on the sidelines, the plan literally was laughed to death in the House. Thereafter, the Legislature almost ignored the governor's tax recommendations, other than his forcing—through threat of veto—the legislators to rescind a two-cent increase in the state tax on gasoline.

Another important aspect of Smith's performance as governor was his congenital lack of diplomacy. Just as he continually harassed newsmen about the way they covered his activities—thus endearing him to them all the more—he also badgered both official and nonofficial guests and visitors about whether they had or had not supported him, had or had not contributed to his campaigns. And, more often than not, Smith could not even remember their names, a flaw that often is fatal to politicians but which Smith managed to overcome with his foot-shuffling, country-boy courtliness.

There was no courtliness, however, in one of Smith's most blatant and politically harmful faux pas. In the spring of 1969, when he had been governor only a few months, Smith was called to Washington for a top-level federal briefing on a new Nixon Administration housing program, which was designed to cope with some slum-housing problems through the use of mobile homes and the freeing of some state-sanctioned funds for investment in low-income housing projects. After the briefing, Smith said he did not approve of the new program— partially because he did not think all slums should be eliminated. "Some people just like to live in slums," he explained, citing as an example his home town of Lubbock where, the governor of the nation's fifth most populous state said, when one slum was eliminated, some of the individuals living there simply moved across the city and started a new slum.

This was the same governor who had promised in his 1969 inaugural address—just a few months before—that he would cope fairly and justly with "problems of the young, of the old, of racial minorities, of disadvantaged economic groups, problems of the sick, the afflicted, and the mentally ill."

On the other hand, Preston Smith always appeared to put a new political twist on the Emersonian epigram about foolish consistency—sometimes in the day-to-day sense that Emerson had in mind.* And if he did not perform as governor with grace, at least he did it with his own individual style.

Smith was not a colorful political figure, despite his polka-dot ties. He was not a cameo politician, and for that reason he studiously avoided television appear-

*"A foolish consistency is the hobgoblin of little minds, adored by little statesmen and philosophers and divines . . . Speak what you think now in hard words and tomorrow speak what tomorrow thinks in hard words again, though it contradict everything you said today."—Ralph Waldo Emerson.

ances whenever possible. He was, in fact, a rather plain man with a quick mind, a pleasant smile on a sturdy face, and a warm handshake, who became governor because he smiled at and shook hands with more Texas voters than probably any governor since W. Lee "Pappy" O'Daniel. An anachronism, as well as a paradox, in his political techniques, he plodded along in the old-fashioned way, his goals as firmly in mind as if he were still a country boy reading about the impeached Governor Jim Ferguson while steering a pair of mules down the rows of cotton.

As governor, Smith was not entirely trusted by anyone—not by liberals or conservatives, not by business nor labor—and, in turn, trusted few people himself. His independence bothered them; their self-interest bothered him. His crudeness and lack of sophistication bothered them; their city-slicker flashiness bothered him.

That is not to say he was without financial support from the wealthy Texas businessmen who always have financed conservative Democratic campaigns, particularly the oil, gas, and banking interests. The business lobbyists who contributed to Smith's campaigns regarded the money as well spent, because they could count on Smith's spending the money wisely—and on the campaign, not to enrich himself personally—as he did with his own hard-earned semifortune.

It is to say, rather, that as a politician Smith relied mostly on his own human resources—chiefly, the ability to make what he considered business-type but fair decisions and the courage to see things through his own mind, even if the result was different from what others saw.

CHAPTER SIX

Gus Mutscher

Gus Franklin Mutscher, throughout his political career and most centrally as speaker of the House, had one primary motto: "Never quit politicking and never underestimate your opponent."

As the Sixty-Second Texas Legislature convened January 12, 1971, most calculated observers had to admit that Mutscher had followed his motto to the letter. Never in history had a House speaker—the most powerful state official not elected statewide—taken his office so seriously or worked so hard at the job, full-time and year-around, for the same paltry $4,800-a-year salary that all other 149 House members received. And though he sometimes had overestimated his opponents, up to that time he had never underestimated them.

Mutscher had not, in fact, ever quit politicking since he was graduated from high school. Even as he entered his second term as speaker in January, 1971, he continued to politick. Assuming everyone was reelected in perpetuity, he had enough "pledges" from incumbent House members to win reelection as speaker overwhelmingly in 1973 (which would have been an unprecedented third consecutive term) and from at least a majority to win the 1975 speaker's race, too.

All of those dreams would turn to ashes some 37 weeks later, but at the time Mutscher was king of the House road. He had struggled and promised and cajoled and threatened his way to a power over the House that no one—not even Mutscher's predecessor, Ben Barnes—had exercised before. He had done it all, essentially, by following his own motto.

It may not be surprising, perhaps, to know in retrospect that Mutscher's ascendancy to and performance as speaker were based in large measure on that one rather simplistic precept. Mutscher was not unintelligent despite his square-faced countenance. He had a mind somewhat above average in capacity and well above average in tenacity. But he was a simple man in the sense that he accepted the homespun axioms, verities, and cliches of his background without question, and then applied them with strong will and plain hardheadedness.

Mutscher came by his strong-mindedness and hardwork life style naturally. He was a farm boy in what could only be described today as poverty-stricken circumstances. Born in the tiny Washington county, Texas, German community called William Penn on November 19, 1932, he did not really hit the big-time until he went a few miles south to Brenham for high school and college in the late 1940's and early 1950's. By that time, he was a practiced farmer's son who also had worked in the Blue Bell Creameries and in other part-time jobs. In short, he knew what he and his community were all about and wanted to get out.

After two years at hometown Blinn Junior College—financed in part by a baseball scholarship (he was a third baseman)—Mutscher set his eyes on the University of Texas. He had been Big Man on Campus at Blinn, but at the University the high point of his stay—other than receiving a business degree and an ROTC commission—apparently was his election as president of Gamma Delta, a Lutheran Church college group. Mutscher also was elected international president of the organization. He sometimes later used this election to describe his own political acumen, because he defeated an incumbent vice-president who was supposed to move up the ladder to the presidency automatically. The parallel must have been painful for him, because many Texas political analysts assumed before the stock-fraud scandal that Mutscher would move up inexorably to the governor's mansion or to Congress.

Two years of Army duty, as a military police officer, might help explain Mutscher's later-revealed sense of control as Speaker of the House of Representatives, where his demands for authority, a chain of command, and stern discipline often were executed with military precision. The Army life also must have honed his interest in money, because he had only been working for the Borden Co. in Houston—as a field representative for sales and advertising—for a year when he started up the conventional ladder of success. He was named, in 1959, as an outstanding young businessman of Harris County by the Chamber of Commerce and the Houston Merchants Association. In the meantime, he was earning more than two years' credit toward a law degree from South Texas College of Law—a program that Mutscher no doubt later wished he had completed.

With that kind of background—two years of business experience in the big city and two years of law school—a young man develops ambition, although this particular young man already had it. Mutscher admitted he was not pressured to make his first race for the Legislature. He did it on his own hook after a sudden inspiration from then-Congressman (now Federal Appeals Judge) Homer Thornberry of Austin, who had asked Mutscher if he would be interested in a Washington job. Instead, Mutscher raised a little money, talked to a lot of people, and defeated incumbent State Representative Sanford Schmidt of Shelby in 1960.

By the time he was 28, then, Mutscher was a member of the Legislature. He was, for the most part, an undistinguished legislator who was loyal in the extreme to successive speakers, Byron Tunnell and Ben Barnes, who were his kind of rural Texas conservatives. Mutscher's only real claim to fame came when Barnes chose him as chairman of the House redistricting committee because Barnes thought Mutscher would work at the job and be more dispassionate about it than most House members. Mutscher earned some kudos on redistricting matters. But he also used his power to eliminate his main rival for speaker, Representative Gene Fondren of Taylor, for whom Mutscher drew a new district that kept Fondren so busy with home-area politics that he fell behind in the speaker's race and finally quit in 1967 to become a railroad lobbyist in Washington. Fondren's departure assured Mutscher's election as speaker in January 1969.

Mutscher also discovered that he had a low-paying job he couldn't really afford, although he was still a bachelor. So even that early in his political life, he began to lean on others for financial support. He did not ask for much at first, but he did ask for it often. Later, the money demands got bigger *and* more frequent as the future speaker's political fortunes increased and, theoretically at least, the need for his time and talent became greater. Despite the money-raising efforts of his Brenham backers, Mutscher's financial needs became so acute and the dollar volume of his spending rose so much that he had to turn for money to Houston. It was not an illogical place for him to search for a pot of gold, since he had worked, albeit as a minor figure, in Houston for two years—a fact that Mutscher later described as "my urban experience."

According to those who financed the sailing of the Mutscher ship, such as Blue Bell Creameries' Ed Kruse, he never failed to serve his angels—from small things such as intervening with state agencies to larger matters such as passing crucial pieces of legislation. All of this was done, to be sure, in the interest of the people he represented; everything he ever did, he said, was in the same interest. In truth, he *did* do things his constituents wanted done—he got more, much more, state money for Blinn Junior College, for example, plus a new state park and a new state school and many other pork-barrel projects of home-area impact.

Mutscher also brought his German-background voters something else, something potentially more important to their cultural sense. He brought them political respectability. Here was one of their own kind who left the William Penn community with a back made strong and hands made calloused by farm labor, who went to college and served his country (post-Korea, pre-Vietnam), who was a success in business, and whose political talents were recognized by his peer-group, which in 1969 and again in 1971 elected him speaker of the House. The folks at home saw that as the penultimate success, for they knew that Gus would *really* be going

Gus Mutscher and Frank Maloney.

places. (Never mind Mutscher's own attitude toward his career, summed up later in the phrase, "I figured with a name like Mutscher I wasn't going anywhere anyway. . . .")

The second-term speaker's popularity with his constituents was so strong that in the spring of 1971, when the heavy stench of scandal was in the air, they continued to lavish praise—and money—on Mutscher. A group of several hundred of the commonfolk were bused to Austin—not at their own expense, for the most part, but at the expense of Mutscher angels—to prove their loyalty at a cocktail party to which all top state officials and Capitol newsmen were invited. A larger group of several thousand later paid the same kind of homage—again, mostly not at their own expense—in a "Speaker's Day" ceremony at Washington-on-the-Brazos State Park.

Mutscher's response to all of this citizen outpouring on his behalf was predictable. Stoutly and almost devoutly maintaining his innocence, as he had done from the first, he struck back at his accusers and said he would stand on his record of achievement. He pointed to his newly formed family (his June, 1969, bride, former Miss America Donna Axum; her daughter Lisa by a previous marriage; and their mutual son Gus Hurley) and said they had been abused by unfeeling political assassins. He leaned on his standard cliches, favoring "good government" and "a progressive legislative program" and representation of "the wishes and desires of all of the people of this good state."

In the spring of 1971, Gus Mutscher was trying his best to ignore the stock-fraud case. He believed from the start that he could ride out the storm of protest against his leadership because he thought the only real source of protest was a disgruntled band of liberals and conservatives, the self-styled Dirty 30. Mutscher looked on his archcritics with more than mere disdain; he considered them despicable as people, worthless as legislators, and incapable as politicians. At the height of attempts by members of the Dirty 30 to force an investigation of the stock-fraud allegations, Mutscher chastised them for being "more interested in passing resolutions than in passing bills." (This remark came at a time when Mutscher was being called "Greedy Gus" by his attackers—a nickname coined by Kountze News editor Archer Fullingon.)

Besides, his small coterie of close lieutenants and floor leaders convinced Mutscher he could hang on to his power as speaker against the then-impotent rebellious minority. That was, of course, what he most wanted to hear.

This view was not unanimous among those on whom Mutscher previously had leaned for advice and money. Several lobbyists and some of his House colleagues, for example, tried to talk him into an early confessional and appointment of an exculpating committee—to come clean with the House, make a Richard Nixon-style "Checkers" speech, and then name a panel that would, after a brief investigation, duly report that the speaker was innocent of any wrongdoing. Mutscher rejected this suggestion, which was not pressed on him strongly anyway, and took the course most of his legislative advisors recommended.

The tide of protest in the House did not abate, but during the legislative session never became strong enough to force Mutscher out of office. Mutscher eventually *was* pressured into creating, prematurely, the House General Investigating committee, with explicit orders to probe the stock-fraud scandal. Although he stacked the five-man committee with some of his most intimate and influential supporters, the committee postponed any significant inquiry until after Mutscher and two of his right-hand men—staff aide Rush McGinty and Representative Tommy Shannon of Fort Worth— had been indicted by the Travis County grand jury on September 23, 1971. By then. it was impossible for the committee to absolve Mutscher in the stock-fraud case.

In the meantime, other than appointing a blatantly friendly and clearly not impartial investigating committee, Mutscher ran the House in the only way he knew—with an iron hand that hammered out pieces of silver for his pals and knots on the head for his enemies. In the early days of the session, Mutscher knew he easily controlled more than 110 of the 150 House members' votes. So he could do literally almost anything he wanted to, for his friends or against his foes, and get away with it.

One of Mutscher's early-session targets, for instance, was not a member of the Dirty 30 but a member of the speaker's own wedding party—Representative Rayford Price of Palestine, a rural conservative like Mutscher.

Price had initiated, during the 1969 session, a campaign for the speakership—contingent on Mutscher's stepping down, whenever that was. Price at the time was Mutscher's chairman of the powerful State Affairs committee, was the only House member asked to participate in the speaker's wedding, and, to many outside observers, was the anointed heir to Mutscher. Price's "iffy" and perhaps premature speakership campaign was based on the widespread rumor that Mutscher would be appointed chief lobbyist for the Texas Brewers Institute when his long-time friend, Homer Leonard, retired.* But Mutscher went before the House to say he intended to be speaker "several more years" and wanted an end to the speakership campaigns by Price and others.

Price's campaign ground to a public halt, although he continued to talk to House members privately about supporting him when Mutscher finally quit. Those conversations continued sub rosa until the 1971 session opened. Then, in a show of muscle to indicate the fate of "traitors," Mutscher summarily dismissed Rayford Price as part of the leadership team, stripped him of the State Affairs committee chairmanship (a job that frequently leads to higher office), and relegated him to minor assignments that would guarantee Price's obscurity and impotence.

Price retaliated in a way Mutscher could understand —he resurrected his speakership campaign publicly and said Mutscher himself would be the main issue in the 1973 speaker's race. This may have reflected some fore-

*Mutscher, who was always close to the business lobby, particularly to the beer lobby, would have been a perfect candidate for the job. Instead, it went to Representative R. H. "Dick" Cory of Victoria, who in 1969 was the speaker's top strategist and House manipulator, as well as head of Mutscher's brain trust.

sight because at the time Price went public with his anti-Mutscher speakership campaign, the stock-fraud scandal was making headlines but had not reached the proportions that would threaten Mutscher's future. It is interesting to note, though, that Price voted with Mutscher's team most of the legislative session; he never attempted to identify himself with the Dirty 30 or to carve out a specific reform niche of his own.

To replace Price as chairman of the State Affairs committee, Mutscher turned to Representative Jim Slider of Naples.

State Affairs is one of the "speaker's" committees, in the sense that the speaker must control it more tightly than other committes and must have absolute power of life or death over the vast array and heavy volume of legislation assigned to it. He must control it because in practice, the State Affairs committee is the graveyard for bills that the business lobby (and therefore usually the speaker) want killed. It is also the greased skid through which quickly slip those measures that the business lobby want passed.

Slider fit perfectly into the Mutscher leadership. He is a salty-tongued rural conservative, a believer in old-style brass-knucks and pork-barrel politics, making up in shrewdness and perspicacity what he lacks in formal education. Slider, a small-town businessman by trade, is a loyalist by nature. He served Mutscher loyally, rarely questioned the speaker's wisdom, and expected to be served in return.

One of the things Slider apparently expected was Mutscher's blessings as speaker-successor. But Slider, like Price before him, learned the hard way what Mutscher meant by loyalty: Toward the end of the 1971 regular session, Slider launched a ten-hour speakership campaign—again, contingent on Mutscher's stepping down—that ended in humiliation when Mutscher sternly ordered him to give back the dozen or so pledges Slider had collected. After apologizing unnecessarily, Slider gave them back and said he had not meant to embarrass Mutscher. Part of the reason for Mutscher's action may have been an earlier Slider comment, typical for its candor and lack of impact judgment, on the stock-fraud case. In an interview about the possibility of his succeeding Mutscher, Slider steadfastly maintained his loyalty to the speaker and added, "The only thing Gus is guilty of is maybe a little greed for trying to make a fast buck." That crack was the kind of unsophisticated, naive behavior that even Mutscher learned to abhor, the more so when it was exhibited by members of his inner circle.

Slider, then, was as pliant and cooperative as other members of the Mutscher "team." But the team was an odd litter of cats, at best. Team members ranged from the knife-them-in-the-back style of Bill Heatly, known as the Duke of Paducah, the one-man king of state spending, to the urbane-and-witty stiletto style of Hilary Doran, a young Del Rio Bourbon out of the early 20th Century; from the oracular and self-confidently intelligent Jim Nugent of Kerrville to the country-slicker, but insightful Dean Cobb of Dumas. There were "Mutscher mafia" men like Delwin Jones of Lubbock, Dick Slack of Pecos, John Traeger of Seguin, and Charlie Jungmichel of La Grande. But there also were juridical-proceduralists like De Witt Hale of Corpus Christi and Menton Murray of Harlingen.

Close to the team, but not totally part of it because of their larger roles, were two men whom Mutscher may have relied on most—Tommy Shannon, the Fort Worth insurance man turned almost full-time aide to Mutscher, and Rush McGinty, a wealthy and ambitious west Texan who kept the books on Mutscher's financial-political accounts. Shannon handled Mutscher's political and administrative dirty work with as much finesse as any man could. McGinty's job was to keep the cards, cash, and checks flowing into the speaker's office—in part to pay for the $5,000 or so a month in Mutscher expenses that the state budget did not anticipate. And, of course, both Shannon and McGinty were indicted with Mutscher on the charge of conspiracy to accept a bribe.

Mutscher later would say he got in on the bank loan-stock purchase deal, with its implied guarantee of profits, in order to pay for an airplane to meet his obligations as speaker and to make himself "financially independent" of the business lobby's special interests, which he had served so long and with such dedication. In a moment of uncharacteristic honesty, on the other hand, McGinty said the deal was arranged to "make money for all of us—what other reason could there be?"

As odd a collection as the Mutscher team may have been, however, it was effective. Time after time, all during the 1971 legislative session, it beat back attempts to undermine the speaker's leadership, while succeeding in doing what Mutscher wanted done.

One of the things Mutscher wanted done, of course, was to get rid of as many of his critics as possible. He contributed much of the effort himself, as an experienced hand in the redistricting game. But he left the mechanics to Delwin Jones of Lubbock, a deceptively quiet and adept hatchet man who, when he was not serving Mutscher, was a farmer. With Mutscher's "guidelines" firmly in mind, Jones went to work chopping up the 150-member House into districts designed to reduce the anti-Mutscher forces by as much as half in the 1973 session—an act not dissimilar to a farmer's spraying DDT on unwanted insects.

The Mutscher-Jones enemy elimination bill was an initial success. It reeked of gerrymander and was justified with classic sophistry, but it did the trick—such as creating an entirely new and politically infeasible central Texas district that threw Representatives Charles Patterson of Taylor, John Bigham of Temple, and Dan Kubiak of Rockdale together. Their mutual sin, suffice it to say, was opposing Mutscher. Unfortunately for the Mutscher team, the Texas Supreme Court found the House redistricting bill blatantly unconstitutional and turned over the job of drawing new districts to a five-man constitutional board, of which Mutscher was a completely inconsequential member.

It was one of the very few genuine defeats Mutscher suffered before he was indicted. And it certainly was not caused by a lack of team effort and support. Indeed, in the war against Mutscher's nerves, the speaker never lost a major fight on his own battleground—the House that he guided so willfully, skillfully, and completely.

So if it can be argued that Mutscher did not violate

his central motto—"never quit politicking and never underestimate your opponent"—it also can be argued that he did not count on having the Securities and Exchange Commission as an opponent. Because with the SEC, the politicking did no good and the time for estimating the enemy agency was two years earlier. Furthermore, Mutscher did finally underestimate an opponent, or more properly two opponents—the Dirty 30 and the public opinion its members aroused against the speaker.

CHAPTER
SEVEN

Ben Barnes

Ben Barnes is totally and completely a political ani-
mal. No one in Barnes' close circle of friends or on his
staff disagree. How could they? From 1960 on, all of his
adult life, politics occupied almost every waking moment—and his dreams as well. Nearly all of his close
friends have been politicians or interested in the art of
government; his social life has been the campaign trail,
the receptions, the dinner meetings, the fund-raising
activities and speaking engagements ad infinitum; his
work has been the affairs of state and tending to constituents' needs; and even his relaxation has served only
as a short breather before the next public demand. Putting it another way rather grandiosely and in a national
context, former President Lyndon Johnson explained
Barnes' track record and life-style pattern on August
14, 1970: "I genuinely believe that Ben Barnes has what
it takes to carry him as far as his ambition will carry
him."

Yet in January, 1971, the stock-fraud scandal threatened to abort this promising career, to smear his reputation and damage his popularity. No matter that he
was not named as having received one of Frank Sharp's
quick-profit bank loan-stock purchase deals, Barnes and
some other state leaders stood guilty before the public
by association. A state senator probably best illustrated
the feeling of Texas toward their elected politicos with
this story: In talking to one of his hometown constituents who was appalled and shocked by "those thieves
in Austin," the senator was wholeheartedly agreeing
with him that the time had arrived to clean up "the
mess" and reform state government. Suddenly, how-

ever, the senator was taken aback by this conversation-stopping question: "Yeh, we're in agreement, senator," the voter commented dryly, "but weren't you there?" Such was also the dilemma faced by Ben Barnes.

Born in the small Comanche County farm community of Comyn—but not in a log cabin—on April 17, 1938, Benny Frank Barnes was the personification of the agrarian myth, the Horatio Alger story, and the American Dream all rolled into one. The elder son of Benjamin Franklin and Ina B. Carrigan Barnes, he had a normal childhood for someone from a poor, depression-ridden West Texas farm area. In other words, since his father believed in the principle of hard work, he became well-acquainted during his school years with such laborious duties as baling hay and hoeing corn; then in the summer he escaped the monotony of the fields and the blistering heat (he has extremely fair skin) by obtaining work as a bricklayer, a milk truck driver, a roughneck in the Kermit oil fields, and even as a miner's helper in Colorado. In many ways, therefore, school was a welcome relief, most definitely a respite from toil and a sanctuary from chores; and accordingly Barnes responded by fashioning a creditable record. At the nearby consolidated DeLeon High School he averaged better than 93 in grades, became president of the newly formed Future Teachers Association, and participated vigorously in athletics, lettering in football, basketball, baseball and track.

Sprouting to 6'3" and a lean 215 pounds, Barnes enrolled at Texas Christian University in the fall of 1956, hopefully to carry on the winning athletic tradition of the Jim Swink era. But an old back injury (actually he had ruptured a disc) prevented him from playing freshman football, from enjoying a closer camaraderie with his friends. And although later laughingly admitting that "the sports world was not deprived of the greatest athlete in the world," he was at the moment deeply discouraged. He therefore began to drift, to exist and function without definite purpose or strong commitment. After one semester he left T.C.U. and enrolled at Tarleton State College during which time he married Martha Jane Morgan, his hometown sweetheart. Again in September, 1957, he changed schools, this time to the University of Texas at Austin, where for two years he strove to attain a degree in business administration. Then he entered the University of Texas Law School in 1959 (under the ninety-hour plan), although not overly enthusiastic in his choice of profession. In the meantime he was working part time as a punch-card operator in the State Health Department, but in order to make ends meet he tried hawking vacuum cleaners from door-to-door at night and on the week-ends. And immediately he was successful. "I sold twelve the first month," he happily recollected, "and made nearly five hundred dollars. But I'll never forget the insults and abuse I took as a door-to-door salesman. I taught me a lot about human nature, and helped me develop the kind of thick hide you've got to have in politics."

From this "Keep Your House Clean" sales venture, Barnes became financially solvent—and possibly developed the independence necessary to blow the whistle on four or five assistants to the Public Health Commissioner who were fattening their own pockets at public and employee expense. And by so doing, by causing a legislative investigation and becoming aware of the processes of government, Barnes found out what excited him, what stirred his ambition, what he wanted to do. No question about it, politics was the only game in town for him. Early in 1960 he announced for the state Legislature and, at age twenty-one, ran against one of the most respected men in Brownwood who, as president of the Chamber of Commerce, seemed to have commitments, Barnes recalled, "from everyone in the district." But it did not matter; Barnes had the desire, the energy, the dedication, the boyish good looks and enthusiasm—and he loved every minute of the campaign. In the three counties "under attack" he reportedly shook everybody's hand twice. "I got up every morning at 4:30 and went to bed at 11:30 or 12:00 at night," he explained. "That's how I won."

Nor did Barnes basically ever change this campaign strategy. In running for each elective office, whether for representative or lieutenant governor or governor, he always wanted to meet the people, shake their hands, impress and persuade them through personal confrontation, give them what several political observers have called "the Ben Barnes treatment." Nor did his stamina and enthusiasm lessen. "Crowds excite him," Richard West, his press secretary, exclaimed. "They're like a catalyst." So Barnes continues to drive himself and his staff relentlessly, increasing work hours as an election nears.

And surely few could fault this success formula, which proved its impact during the 1960's. Immediately upon entering the Legislature in 1961, Barnes backed Wade Spilman for speaker and lost. But in receiving his lumps of defeat that session, he was forced to learn the complex workings of the House, the intricate maneuverings of parliamentary procedure, as well as the hard lesson that the "outs" could accomplish very little. Hence he thereafter selected his candidates more carefully and prepared more thoroughly. Two years later he was a driving force in electing Byron Tunnel as speaker, and at twenty-three was rewarded with the chairmanship of the Rules committee, one of the most powerful committees in the House. Then late in 1964, upon receiving advance notice of Tunnel's appointment to the Railroad Commission from his close friend Governor John Connally, Barnes set up a command post in the Commodore Perry Hotel—with ten to fifteen phones— and carried out "Operation Blitzkrieg." Together with such fellow representatives as David Crews of Conroe, Jim Slider of Naples, Randy Pendleton of Andrews, and Bill Clayton of Springlake, he marshaled his pledge cards of several years in the future for the January session, and within thirty-six hours had a majority of the House supporting him for speaker. So in 1965 Barnes, the youngest person (at twenty-six) ever to preside over the House, amazed the old pros with his adroitness and finesse and political know-how. In fact, for the next four years the "Connally protege" carried out the governor's program, adeptly manipulating both the House and Senate. Consequently, no one was surprised when he was elected lieutenant governor in 1968 and re-elected in 1970; for already he was being hailed as the fair-haired young man of Texas politics.

But with each legislative session, with every crisis in decision-making, Barnes caused deep resentment and created formidable opposition. Like any politician who has held office for any length of time, he offended a number of people, stepping on their toes once too often, thus nurturing their undying hatred. Hence during the 1968-72 period especially, Texans were fed a constant stream of propaganda by both his friends and enemies alike, one group ascribing to him all the virtues of a modern-day savior and the other maligning him as a crook, a lecher, and someone to be feared.

Barnes, however, was much too complex an individual for such simple solutions. For instance, few people disputed that he had charisma, that he was canny and bright, that he had the ability to inspire, even command, unquestioned admiration and devotion. During the 1971 session any number of state senators such as Bill Moore of College Station, Don Kennard of Fort Worth, J. P. Word of Meridian, and Joe Christie of El Paso (just to name a few) testified frequently to his leadership ability and his fairness. Others were equally impressed with his instincts, under pressure, to make judgment calls both incisively and decisively. Still others appreciated his great sense of loyalty to his friends, even though in such cases as Frank Erwin, the controversial University of Texas regent, it hurt him with the intellectual community.* But everyone always marveled at his ability to meet with people, to put them at ease, to make the most simple conversation appear to be meaningful dialogue. "I was flattered," a young Austinite admitted after meeting him for the first time. "He read me real fast. He instinctively seemed to know that to impress me would be for him to act like he was listening to what I had to say and treat me like an intelli-

*Although a close personal friend and often named as one of Barnes' top political advisers, Erwin has not been a confidante either on political affairs or day-to-day decisions of the state in the last few years. In regard to matters concerning The University of Texas and higher education, however, he has definitely been influential. Barnes' detractors have always claimed that when Erwin pulled the strings, Barnes would hop. But since becoming lieutenant governor, Barnes appears to have shed most, if not all, of the Connally-Erwin strings.

gent human being." His executive assistant, Robert Spellings, who obviously considered Barnes to be the greatest thing since sliced bread and night baseball, explained: "He's got the greatest ability in the world of taking two people with completely divergent and opposing views on an issue and of bringing them from left and right to a middle area."

By exuding utmost confidence, Barnes also was able to instill faith in his capabilities and his program for Texas. Rather pragmatically he prided himself, since his speakership days, in finding out, he candidly stated in January, 1972, "what the major problems are, what the priorities are, and trying to solve those problems without real regard to a political philosophy." Believing that state government had become increasingly inefficient, he was convinced that progressive legislation—a new state constitution, annual legislative sessions, a reorganization of the executive branch, a cabinet system of government—was necessary "to deliver services to the people," to meet the demands of urban Texas. And the only way to do so "is through leadership," he concluded. "I think history has produced from time to time people who have been able to ignite the spark of enthusiasm . . . to get people to really work together . . . for a common purpose and common goal." Probably Senator Oscar Mauzy best described Barnes' thinking and actions by saying: "He is not in a philosophical straitjacket which will prevent him from considering any new or innovative ideas."

At times, therefore, Barnes was thought of as a master politician, as a young Lyndon Johnson without the rough edges and the accent. He had incredible recall, absorbing statistical information in computer-like fashion; consequently, he impressed those who came in contact with him. He also had excellent intuitive judgment regarding popular moods, gleaning and registering comments from literally thousands of people. Yet, he checked out his feelings scientifically, being a firm believer in public opinion polls. But, most amazing, he was unbelievably introspective. In the presence of a few trusted friends and reporters he coldbloodedly—and sometimes mercilessly—analyzed himself almost as if

he were sitting on the other side of a two-way mirror
and watching a puppet of himself perform. In this same
manner, one political correspondent observed, "Barnes
can make a gut decision, come up with a rationale for it,
plan a strategy to carry it out, and then, even in the
process of its being carried out, pick the thing apart
and say, 'This was a mistake. This was a good coup.
And we should have followed this up.' "

During twelve years of public service Barnes followed a success formula in politics, a pattern established
by other sagacious and victorious state leaders. Of
course, the primary objective was to win, because few
men in American history have been able to afford Henry
Clay's campaign philosophy, "I'd rather be right than
president"—and therefore he was "right" three times.
But once in power Barnes adopted rules of action, many
of which merit closer scrutiny for those who aspire to
high office.

Probably the most unique is the Rule of Yes. During
a legislative session the Senate considers at least 2,000
bills, with an average of ten people per measure asking
the lieutenant governor for help. So, except to prepos-
terous proposals or those which he has publicly opposed, Barnes said "yes" to each of these people on the
theory that hopefully a majority would get what they
wanted; that to another 20 or 30 per cent he could place'
the blame for defeat on the opposition; and that to the
rest, *c'est la vie.* Barnes himself couched the Rule of
Yes in more pragmatic terms. During the 1971 session,
he claimed, he would give any bill "a run" as soon as
he received a list of twenty-one senators (a two-thirds
majority) who tentatively were supporting it. He therefore placed the responsibility to obtain the necessary
votes on different pressure groups, thereby—according
to Barnes—saving valuable Senate time. Meanwhile, he
applied the Rules of Yes to people inquiring about the
status of particular bills. Whatever its moral ramifica-
tions, the Rule of Yes was one of Barnes' most effective
personal political strategies.

Equally important was the Barnes rule concerning
finances. Lyndon Johnson supposedly advised Barnes
to be as liberal as possible without offending or disturb-

ing his money base. In other words, one high state official commented understandably and in agreement, "stay with the guys who have the cash and you can do whatever else you need to do in terms of media and campaigning." For anyone who plans to run a statewide campaign, especially in Texas, and who may aspire to national recognition and leadership in the Democratic Party, this idea deserves careful consideration.

And lastly, in regard to decision-making, Barnes acknowledged that former President Johnson had given him sound advice. "When you've got a tough decision to make and when both sides are after you tooth and tong," Barnes earnestly exclaimed to the authors, "get off by yourself and decide what you think is best for the people ten or twenty years from now, because it's going to be you that has to live with the decision and not those who are hammering at you."

Because of his charisma and potential as a politician, and because of his close friendship with such men as Johnson and Connally and Erwin (the so-called Establishment), Barnes was a favorite topic of public debate, probably more than any other state official in recent years. For instance, stories about his sex life, about his feminine conquests, are legion. As with other prominent political figures in history, the proverbial tale of a hushed-up paternity suit made the rounds. Then because of his divorce in 1970, there was gossip for a time that Martha, his former wife, could no longer endure his indiscretions. Yet they parted seemingly without animosity and, after Martha remarried first, daughter Amy decided to live with her and son Gregg with him. But the most effective method of discrediting him, his detractors found, was political lampooning and humor. In no way could he fight the nickname of "Bedroom Ben," who was reportedly "the fastest zipper in the West," nor combat the automobile bumper stickers (lampooning the television announcement: "It's 10:30. Do you know where your children are?") issued by his enemies: "It's 10:30. Do you know where your lieutenant governor is?" Nor could he retort to Cactus Pryor's comment at the Headliners Club stag luncheon in 1971 that he was trying to emulate Will Rogers. After all,

Ben Barnes and Lyndon B. Johnson.

Pryor joked, "Will Rogers never met a man he didn't like and Barnes never met a woman that . . ." In fairness to Barnes, however, the reader should note that not one of his enemies or political opponents ever substantiated any of these charges. Yet some political observers attributed his near loss of Travis County in the November election of 1970 almost exclusively to such rumors. But other factors, such as state employees registering their unhappiness with existing state government as well as Republican opponent Byron Fullerton being an Austin resident and a University of Texas law professor, may also have been important.*

In similar fashion political enemies harped on, and made much of, Barnes' financial status. After the stock-fraud scandal erupted and the Senate was proposing an ethics bill, any number of people urged him to "reveal all" so that the public might have confidence in at least one state leader. The *Texas Observer* was particularly aggressive and persistent; yet not until May 21, 1971, was a detailed statement forthcoming. And immediately many journalists intimated a credibility gap; for Robert Spellings, who prepared and filed this financial statement, listed Barnes' net worth at $83,621.20, although it was public knowledge that Barnes had business interests in radio stations at Grand Prairie and Abilene, several Holiday Inns, a multi-million-dollar shopping center and an apartment complex in Brownwood, numerous stock investments, and 863 acres in valuable farm land. For someone who had worked for the state all of his adult life (at $400 a month) such circumstantial evidence was damning. Certain reporters also questioned Spellings' accounting procedures, suggesting that a listing of all assets and liabilities, then a subtracting of one from the other, was not only standard procedure but would have been more understandable to the average citizen and theefore less deceptive.**

*In Travis County, Barnes beat Fullerton 35,104 to 33,252. Statewide, Barnes defeated Fullerton 1,497,515 to 750,445.

**Barnes' financial disclosure statement reflected assets of $267,721.72 and liabilities of $184,100.52, yielding a net worth of $83,621.20. The Dallas Morning News reported that if Barnes had used "the more conventional accounting approach of listing

In reply, Spellings maintained that Barnes had been open and candid—if not too candid. In fact, many Barnes advisors were against any financial disclosure, lest it in some way give "ammunition" to the enemy. But Barnes was adamant, Spellings asserted, about "hiding nothing"; therefore, he filed a statement in May, 1971, and then responded further to a series of questions in the Houston *Chronicle* on January 9, 1972.*

Actually, Barnes was financially dependent on Herman Bennett, a multi-millionaire contractor from Brownwood who looked upon him like an only son and who was described as a "financial fairy godfather" by the Dallas *Morning News.* "It's that pure and simple," Spellings exclaimed. "If he didn't have Herman Bennett to support him, he could not hold public office." Yet, surprisingly, Bennett disliked politics and had urged Barnes to get out of the political rat-race. Rather graphically, Barnes put it this way: "I think you can draw the comparison between Bennett wanting me out of politics and a mother wanting a son home from Viet Nam."

As for Barnes' somewhat controversial financial statement, Spellings staunchly defended his action: "If I were just trying to get someone like my wife to understand what all Barnes' assets were and all his liabilities were, I agree with you. What I probably should have done would have been to have listed all of his assets over here and all his liabilities over there. But the accounting principle I used . . . is the most widely accepted form used by businessmen and investors."

So for Barnes, who had become inured to innuendoes and accusations, the stock-fraud scandal was just one more in a long series of hazardous situations to "sweat out" and endure. Never one to let others decide his fate, however, he began campaigning for governor immediately after the close of the 1971 legislative session in June. And why? To him the answer was prag-

assets and liabilities separately," his financial statement would have shown assets of $436,346.72 and liabilities of $352,725.52.

*In answer to one of Bo Byers' questions, Barnes stated that his gross income, as reported on his 1970 federal tax return, was $57,436.74. He also admitted that Herman Bennett had consolidated and paid off most of his debts.

matic and clear. For the previous eleven years he had been an avid student of government, undoubtedly as well informed as anyone in the state on financing, the legislative process, and the day-to-day operations of every state agency. As Speaker of the House and then as Lieutenant Governor, he had also performed brilliantly at times under continuous pressure, with a maturity far out of proportion to his age. In other words, he candidly stated, "I have trained and gotten ready to be governor—and I think that's important."

Yet in the Ben Barnes story there may be portents of tragedy. At thirty-four he was an "old" politician. For almost twelve years he campaigned so hard and became so deeply involved in state affairs that the system exacted a heavy price from him. For he surely had not had time to read as widely or attain as much educational training as he would have liked. And although having already received many high honors and much adulation, he had been subjected to the destructive forces which elective officials have increasingly been experiencing from the public. Although he was investigated and cleared by the SEC, the FDIC, the FBI, and the Internal Revenue, he still had to face such remarks as that expressed in a Kountze *News* editorial on January 20, 1972: "With Pious Preston and Bedroom Ben joined by Dolph Briscoe in the Governor's race the only choice facing the people of Texas is between two crooks and a legislator out of the 1950s who pushes wetbacks on his vast South Texas landholdings. The people of Texas deserve better than that."

How ironical it was, then, that Barnes, who had worked for twelve years in government and had trained himself specifically for the governorship, might find that the innuendoes and guilt by association over the stock fraud scandal—although he was not centrally involved and although no charges of any kind were filed against him—would form the greatest threat yet to his remarkable career.

CHAPTER EIGHT

The Dirty 30

It would be a gross historical distortion to deal with the spring, 1971, stock-fraud furor without putting at least a brief political spotlight on that motley band of malcontents who called themselves, rather proudly, the Dirty 30. For it was the Dirty 30 more than any other element—including the SEC and the press—which kept the stock-fraud case alive as a political issue through the spring and into the summer. Perhaps more importantly in the long run, it was the Dirty 30 that put a crucial focus on the political aspects of the case: how "the system" as operated by Speaker Gus Mutscher did not merely *allow* but fundamentally *assumed* the kind, if not the magnitude, of pernicious machinations that the SEC charged were behind the House portion of the stock-fraud scandal.

No one would seriously argue that the Dirty 30 ever was or could be a viable political force. It was a spontaneous, politically unnatural collection of the urban and the rural, the Democrat and the Republican, the liberal and the conservative. It was no more than what it purported to be during the 1971 legislative session—a group of dissimilar individuals who, for various reasons, opposed the reign and the rule of the Mutscher team and who fought, however ineffectively, for procedural reforms and ethical standards that would weaken the Mutscher team's, or any team's, control over the legislative process.

Similarly, no one would seriously argue that the members of the Dirty 30 were consummate legislators. Their combined production of bills and resolutions was remarkable minuscule, even counting local and uncontested bills. Their contribution was limited in part, to be sure, by the very fact of their opposition to Mutscher. He simply did not let them have a chance to pass many measures, on the traditional ground that you do not invite your enemies to your own feast. But there is ample evidence that, at least in the spring of 1971, the Dirty 30 would not have been a particularly productive group, in terms of legislation, even if it had been given full access to the lawmaking mechanism.

These men and one woman did not have any claim to heroic lawmaking status and they were unlikely to coalesce again in the future as they did in Gus Mutscher's spring of despair. Still, they did something that no one else was doing at the time. They kept the public aware that there were unanswered questions about the role of state officials in the stock-fraud case and that recurrences of the whole mess could only be avoided by thorough reform of both the legislative process and the ethical climate in which the laws are made.

That one function distinguished the 1971-model Dirty 30 from the earlier models (which in the 1960's were invariably all-liberal minorities) and probably will make a repeat performance both impossible and unnecessary. Unnecessary because it is a virtual certainty that a newly urban-dominated House in 1973 will enact the kind of reforms advocated by the Dirty 30. Impossible because it is almost as certain that in the 1970's urban liberal Democrats and Republicans will make political progress sufficient to render a single minority coalition untenable.

But even if it planted the seeds of its own destruction, the Dirty 30 of 1971 vintage earned something of a place in Texas political history, not so much because of *what* it was as *where*. It became an axiom of sorts among political reporters that any given Dirty 30 press conference would be boring, almost devoid of "hot" copy due to the coalition's lack of public relations sense. Yet the Dirty 30 members succeeded in getting their message across to the public, precisely because at that time they were in the middle of the only real political fight over the stock-fraud case—the hassle with Gus Mutscher over the charges and their meaning.

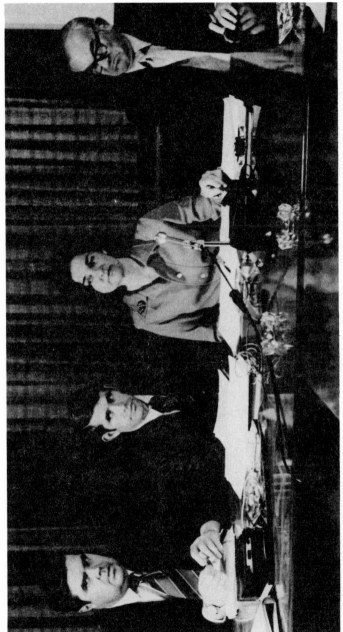

Representatives Allred, Denton, Farenthold, and Moore at a Dirty Thirty press conference in the Spring of 1971.

Members of the Dirty 30 started the session by picking at Mutscher's control system, and they kept it up all spring. They were disappointed, in a way, when Mutscher finally capitulated, agreed to an investigation, and then named five of his close House lieutenants to the committee charged with making the investigation. The committee members were all chairmen of other Mutscher-appointed committees: Menton Murray of Harlingen, higher education; Jim Nugent of Kerrville, rules; Jim Slider of Naples, state affairs; DeWitt Hale of Corpus Christi, judiciary; and Clyde Haynes of Vidor, labor.

It was only a temporary psychological defeat for the Dirty 30, however, and not really a setback to the reform program in general. Because the transparency of Mutscher's investigation was so blatant that even some of his friends complained privately. "I'd damned sure like for my clients to be able to pick their juries," a lawyer loyal to the speaker grumbled. "I'd have the best acquittal record in the world." So for the Dirty 30's educational effort, Mutscher's appointment of the committee—officially on April 13, 1971, eighty-five days after the stock-fraud suit was filed in Dallas—actually was beneficial. It reflected what the Dirty 30 saw as the speaker's arrogant unwillingness to permit serious scrutiny of the SEC's charges.

In truth, Mutscher probably was rational, if also self-serving, in his opposition to some of the Dirty 30 investigation proposals. Representative Frances Farenthold of Corpus Christi, the only woman in the House and one of the Dirty 30 leaders, sponsored a resolution, for instance, that would have created a committee solidly stacked against Mutscher and his co-investors and that would have armed the committee with fervently hostile instructions about the investigation. Mutscher obviously fought the Farenthold resolution—and successfully, as he won a classic vote of 118 to 30 on March 15. That was precisely two weeks before Mutscher allowed the House to create the House General Investigating committee and, simultaneously, to instruct the Attorney General to head a parallel study by a group of public officials and private citizens. Neither panel set any records for diligence or effectiveness.

But Mutscher fought just as strenuously against relatively meaningless and innocuous investigation proposals. A prime example was a resolution by Representative Neil Caldwell of Alvin, which immediately after the stock-fraud case was filed asked the state officials named in the SEC suit, including the speaker, to come before the House and explain their involvement. Mutscher won the fight against that resolution, too—110 to 35 on February 16, on a vote made more lopsided than it would have been if it had not come so early in the session. Two months later, as public indignation over the case continued to mount, probably even Mutscher would have voted for the mild Caldwell resolution if he had thought it would satisfy the public. Instead, the speaker buried the Caldwell proposal in a subcommittee chaired by Representative R. B. McAlister of Lubbock—who had introduced Mutscher to his future wife, Donna Axum.

When the time finally came for Mutscher to cave in and create his own investigation, the speaker did so with a characteristic slap at both the Dirty 30 and the press, which he saw as the Dirty 30's only ally.

"The air must be cleared once and for all," Mutscher intoned. "The publicity surrounding the current SEC activities must be fully explored." (The careful reader will note that Mutscher only specified that the "publicity" about the SEC's probe should be fully explored.) He added, "I want the members of this House and the people of this state to know the facts. Facts—not rumors—not innuendos, not distortions. I want to emphasize that I do not want the results of these resolutions . . . to be a whitewash nor a witch-hunt."

Mutscher later would lay the same kind of opprobrium on the Dirty 30 in both general and specific terms. He told the Speaker's Day crowd, composed largely of business lobbyists and his own constituents, that he questioned the motives of "anyone who seeks only personal display and self-advancement" and that he was trying to do his job "in the face of discord and distortion." The speaker asserted, "Frankly, there are those who have tried to enhance their political stature at the expense of mine."

Finally, on May 30, 1971, the next-to-last day of the regular session, Mutscher struck out frontally and specifically at the Dirty 30.

Members of that group, still angered by the "Mutschermandering" House redistricting bill passed the day before, retaliated in part by refusing to let the House take up any bills on a so-called local and consent calendar. Some of the bills had major public policy significance and all of them had been held up by Mutscher for last-minute action as a means of keeping his team members in line. The other part of the Dirty 30 protest, therefore, was to object to the speaker's handling of the bills in such a way as to prohibit thorough study and full debate.

After they had knocked the bills off the calendar, Mutscher accused the Dirty 30 members of "irresponsible" and "partisan political action" and said it was typical of their conduct throughout the spring. "This 'temper tantrum' is rather like a child who cannot have the game played his way and then proceeds to tear up everyone's toys," the speaker said in a press release. He then ticked off th bills that Dirty 30 members had killed (temporarily; most of them were passed the next day)—banking law reforms, a crackdown on drug pushers, amendments to strengthen antiobscenity laws, outlawing teen-age common-law marriage, fireman and policeman benefit increases, additional pollution controls, etc. Mutscher's tirade against the Dirty 30 concluded with what must have been on his mind for four months: "This self-styled name seems to have become very appropriate."

Mutscher's speech, in effect, was a session-ending challenge to draw the 1972 battle lines and let loose all the hostilities. The Dirty 30 members responded with hearts full of glee and mouths full of stored-up venom. Most of them had tried for 139 days, often without success, to keep the discussion of Mutscher's role in the stock-fraud case institutional rather than personal—to complain about Mutscher's way of running the system without running down Mutscher as a man. But with

Mutscher's speech, they replied in kind: They called the speaker a dictator, a despot without conscience, a servant of private rather than public interests. They cited a long series of specific acts of reprisal against Mutscher critics—including the redistricting bill that creatively but patently (and, as it turned out, unconstitionally) went out of its way to eliminate enemies of the speaker. And, on the lowest level of personal criticism, the Dirty 30 members began referring to Mutscher and his team in public with the phrase they had used in private for four months—"neo-Hitler and his Nazi pickpockets."

The Dirty 30 coalition had come full cycle between January 12 and May 30. It had started as a small and mostly ignored ethics and reform bunch whose criticisms reeked of carping and nit-picking, a group that tried, perhaps too early, to draw the obvious parallel between Mutscher's involvement in the stock-fraud scandal and the speaker's way of stage-managing the House.*

But by the time the session ended, the Dirty 30 had become the object of a strong Mutscher counterattack— as well as the only publicly and discretely identified source of opposition to Mutscher.

Moreover, through the news media, the public had come to know many of the Dirty 30 members almost personally—a difficult feat for a group that at best contained one-fourth of the 150 House members. And people of diverse backgrounds and political affiliations realized the Dirty 30 was a force to be reckoned with, if only because it represented such an amalgamation of disparate and interesting characters: among others, Tom Moore of Waco, the spell-binding and somewhat demagogic liberal orator from out of the 1950's; "Sissy" Farenthold of Corpus Christi, the mod and morose

---

*Another Dirty 30 tactic was to pass, without debate or objection, a House resolution citing the Boston strangler, Albert DiSalvo, for his contributions to birth control; the public was informed, too, that Mutscher himself passed a 1969 resolution honoring Frank W. Sharp at the same time Sharp was financing Mutscher's quick-profit stock deal. The point of the Dirty 30 move was that Mutscher's House operation kept legislators from knowing what they were doing.

but seriously analytical prophet of doom; Fred Agnich of Dallas, the articulate and thoroughly partisan Republican millionaire with the future on his mind; Bob Gammage of Pasadena and Lane Denton of Waco and Dan Kubiak of Rockdale, quiet former teachers who moved from pedagogy to politics with passion; Zan Holmes of Dallas and Curtis Graves of Houston, the only blacks in the House but with contrasting styles, Holmes the dignified preacher and Graves the showboat phraseologist; Dave Allred of Wichita Falls, the Renaissance man with indisputably decent impulses in his blood; Charles Patterson of Taylor, a congenital conservative who kept asking deep questions about the conventional wisdom; Will Lee, Bill Blythe, E. E. "Sonny" Jones, Jim Earthman, Sid Bowers, and Walter "Mad Dog" Mengden, all conservative Houston Republicans who knew something was wrong but were not quite sure how to change it; Dick Reed of Dallas and R. C. Nichols of Houston, workingmen with the kind of labor-union training that enabled them to speak in plain language to the plain folks (Nichols in 1969 was calling Mutscher "the biggest whore of them all").

Even if the Dirty 30 had failed to become a majority coalition, then, its members had made significant contributions to the public's understanding of the real meaning behind the stock-fraud case.

CHAPTER NINE

The System Defends Itself

"The team" that ran the House did not crumble in the spring of 1971, despite the legal and political problems of Mutscher, Shannon, Heatly, McGinty, and Schulte. In fact, it was something of a tribute to Mutscher's leadership and control that the team members devoutly continued to support the speaker, usually with strong public statements reiterating the traditional American principle that the accused is assumed to be innocent until proven guilty.

That was not an easy position to take. At the time, each day's newspaper contained, if not a new charge against Mutscher, at least a restatement of, or an elaboration on, an earlier accusation. And by early March, newspaper letters-to-the-editor columns and radio-television interview shows were full of indignant citizen responses to the SEC allegations, and most of the public attention was focused on Mutscher. The speaker, after all, was the easiest target. Unlike the governor, he did not have some exculpatory deed to point out, as Smith did with his own veto of Frank Sharp's bank-deposit insurance bills; unlike his aides McGinty and Schulte, Mutscher could not assume the anonymity of behind-the-scenes work; and unlike Shannon and even Bill Heatly, he was a well-known public official far outside the confines of his legislative district. It was in a context of constant criticism, then, that Mutscher and his team operated, even from the early stages of the 1971 legislative session.

Mutscher was not without considerable resources, to be sure. He had campaigned in the districts of most incumbent House members, seeking to make sure that the voters elected representatives who could "work with" the speaker. Having been assured of his own re-election to the House and to the speakership, Mutscher had spent a disproportionate part of the 1970 political year traveling around the state speaking, eating, and politicking on behalf of men he wanted on his team. And, to the amazement of many, he lost very few races in which he took real interest. As a result, his hard core of support—legislators who would do his will almost without regard to their own political futures—was greater during the regular session of the Sixty-second Legislature than that of any speaker in modern times. And no more than a handful of team members quit during the session itself.

Moreover, building on the experience as well as the concept of his Speaker-predecessor Ben Barnes, Mutscher had converted the $400-a-month speakership into a full-time, year-round job and the House staff into a large and politically effective unit. By December, 1971, when the House was not in session and, with a few exceptions, not even functioning as a legislative body, Mutscher had 103 employees on the payroll. The total cost to the taxpayers for this operation was nearly four times as much as it had been seven years earlier, before Barnes became speaker.

Not all of Mutscher's political activities were paid for by the state—again following the Barnes standard. His constituents financed a small part of it, and individuals outside of his district—most of them from Houston—put up some of the money. But most of the additional expenses were covered by contributions from special-interest groups, the so-called "business lobby" that Mutscher served, in his legislative capacity, with such diligence.

So Mutscher, who in many ways as speaker was a special creation of the lobby, faced the 1971 legislative session—even after the stock-fraud scandal was revealed—with a great deal of confidence that his "team" would win the big game. For a while, it appeared that despite the scandal and the attendant public furor, everything would be in the Mutscher mold of "business as usual." At every early opportunity, the omnipotence of the team was demonstrated and reform efforts by the opposition, chiefly the Dirty 30, were smothered. The speaker appeared to control three-fifths of the 150 House members' votes completely, with the ability to call on four-fifths of the members when a critical issue was at stake.

The speaker did not have that kind of support just because he had campaigned for most of the incumbents. He also exercised vast and complex powers over the House—powers that were woven interstitially into what became known to both friend and foe of Mutscher as "the system." More specifically, Mutscher was the broker who translated the desires of the special-interest groups into action, always with the help of the particular group, whether the business lobby or the teacher lobby or the public employees' lobby. The team members actually executed the legislative part of the system, but only on orders from—or with the expressed consent of—the speaker. With few exceptions, the team men never dealt directly with the interest groups; that was Mutschers' job, and that represented a major element in the speaker's control system.

Another major element of Mutscher's vast power was that of making appointments to the forty-seven House committees, including the designation of chairmen, and of referring bills to committees of the speaker's choosing. The two powers were supplemental in nature and traditionally had been considered vital to the speaker's control of the legislative process. If the speaker did not control at least a few key committees—appropriations, taxes, rules, and state affairs, to mention the most important ones—he would be unable to guarantee approval of bills he or his supporters (such as the business lobby) wanted passed, or to guarantee a timely death for bills he or his supporters did not want passed. And if the speaker did not have the power to refer bills to committees of his choice, he similarly would be unable to "deliver." Inherent in the assumptions behind these two corollary powers was that Mutscher would send bills to whatever stacked committee would be most likely to produce the result he and/or the special-interest groups desired.

The final major element in Mutscher's control system was his apparent goal to remain speaker indefinitely. At the start of the 1971 legislative session, he became only the seventh man in history to be elected to a second term as speaker of the Texas House.* In order to keep his troops in line, he still was collecting pledge cards for the 1973 and 1975 sessions. If every 1971 incumbent member of the legislature were re-elected in 1972 and 1974, Mutscher said early in January, 1971, he would be re-elected with two-thirds of the vote in 1973 and with a strong majority in 1975. It was obvious to many of those pledged to Mutscher for future elections that the pledges were more of a re-affirmation of faith in the speaker than an actual commitment to vote for him again. But his use of the pledge cards to perpetuate himself in office had an immediate as well as a long-range purpose—to force upon his constitutionally co-equal colleagues the realization that, in order to keep up good relations with Mutscher, they must continuously pledge their loyalty by pledging their future vote in a future speaker's race. Mutscher was fond of quoting the late U.S. Speaker Sam Rayburn's dictum, "If you want to *get* along, you've got to *go* along."

With all of these resources and tactics at his disposal, then, Gus Mutscher ran the House in a calculated, shrewdly mechanical, and effectively unchallenged way —unchallenged, that is, until the stock-fraud scandal became well-publicized. After news of the scandal was disseminated around the world, Mutscher was challenged on just about everything he did. Most of the time he defeated his opposition by wide margins. But on a few occasions, particularly later in the session, it was

*The Texas speakership produced such 20th century political leaders as United States House Speaker Sam Rayburn, Governor Pat M. Neff, Texas Supreme Court Chief Justice Robert W. Calvert, and United States Senator and Governor Price Daniel. But only four men other than Gus Mutscher were elected to two terms as speaker after the turn of the century: Coke R. Stevenson, 1933-37; Reuben Senterfitt, 1951-55; Waggoner Carr, 1957-61; and Ben Barnes, 1965-69. Prior to that time only two men had been elected to more than one term; the all-time record holder was M. D. K. Taylor, who served in 1859-1861, 1863-1866, and 1873-1874.

close—such as when the team, with all the arm-twisting the entire business lobby could muster, beat a corporate income tax by only 23 votes. He also just barely hustled the votes to pass, with immediate effect, a tax bill that put most of its $622 million burden directly on consumers. On one other occasion it appeared that Mutscher might lose a major battle: the bill appropriating more than $7 billion to finance state government for the next two years.

House passage of the bill had been basically a one-man show for nearly all of the previous decade. The script called for Bill Heatly of Paducah, chairman of the House Appropriations committee, to put the massive 400-page state budget on his colleagues' desks as short a time as possible before it was to be voted on; to explain, unintelligibly, the gross mathematics of the bill; to call on a chosen few of his hand-picked committee members for equally meaningless explanations of each section of the bill; to mumble unresponsive answers to questions; and then to demand immediate passage of the bill. Amendments to the bill were difficult to draw, because of the time factor, and almost pointless to offer, because the amendment sponsor took the chance of offending Heatly permanently on a personal level, which meant the offending party could count on never receiving any pork-barrel projects in his district for the duration of his service in the Legislature.

The control system went even further, because the bill first approved by the House did not necessarily bear any relationship to the final state budget. Heatly, who was as strong-minded as he was venal, always rewrote the bill in a 10-member House-Senate conference committee, anyway, and a conference committee report was not subject to amendment by either the House or the Senate—it had to be either approved or rejected. The conference committee was supposed to be no more than a vehicle for the compromising of differences between House and Senate versions of the same bill. But Heatly, because of his long tenure and his infinite grasp of the way state government "worked," turned the appropriations conference committee process into a final biennial opportunity to help his friends and to wound his enemies, and frequently also to feather his own political nest.*

In 1971, however, there were new challenges to Heatly's autocratic abuse of the appropriations process. Early in the session, on January 20, 1971, Representative John Hannah of Lufkin sought to prohibit the power of the conference committees to add to bills material that had not been approved by either house of the Legislature. That would seem to be a rather obvious and valuable kind of limitation—the kind used by the U.S. Congress, for example—if one accepted the function of a conference committee as a compromising unit between co-equal bodies. Hannah and his supporters made it clear that their goal was to prevent Heatly from writing his own state budget. Heatly, with the all-out backing of Mutscher and the business lobby, quickly knocked down the single most significant reform proposal of the session, 102 to 38.

The reformers were not through with Heatly, however. Upon bringing the appropriations bill before the House on April 22, 1971, Heatly found himself confronted with nearly a hundred amendments—far more than he had dealt with before, many of them dealing, for a change, with major matters of broad public policy. The amendment process was spearheaded by members of the Dirty 30 who with a handful of their staff aides had worked long hours—most of them at night—tearing the appropriations bill into little pieces. It was a heroic endeavor, since the bill was made available to House members only 72 hours before it was to be brought before the House for a vote. Dirty 30 members found hundreds of items of pure pork-barrel politics and blatant political discrimination—such as $220,000 for a moss-cutter on Caddo Lake, but only for that part of

*A 1971 example: Heatly wrote into the appropriations bill, without spelling it out in a way recognizable to anyone else, the sum of $75,000 in taxpayers' money to bring industry to his poverty-stricken dryland-farming district. It may be pointless to add that his district was the only one in the state benefiting from such Heatly generosity, and had been approved neither by the House nor the Senate. Other previously unapproved additions by the Heatly conference committee in 1971 totaled at least $65 million and probably more.

the lake that lay in the district of Healy's friend Jim Slider and not for the part of the lake that lay in the district of Dirty 30 member Ben Z. Grant of Marshall.*

The Dirty 30 and its allies actually offered a total of 69 amendments to the House appropriations bill. Less than a dozen were adopted. But the move had accomplished its two main objectives: to force the House into seriously looking, in detail, at Heatly's initial version of the state budget and to knock permanently from the House mythology the suggestion that Heatly's wisdom should not be challenged frontally.

Early in the session of 1971, with the stock-fraud case already the subject of widespread citizen discussion, the Mutscher team grasped the idea of putting an ethics bill and a pay-raise amendment together in a single proposal for the May 18, 1971, special election on constitutional amendments. (The election had to be held, anyway, because of an emergency over the state's constitutional limitation on welfare spending.) The original inspiration came, predictably, from the so-called Speaker's Committee of 100—a group of 147 persons whose broad responsibilities for recommending improvements in the legislative process included most centrally the task of recommending higher legislative pay. The committee duly reported, a week before the 1971 legislative session began, that legislative salaries should be higher and that the pay level should be set by a constitutionally prescribed commission instead of by a voter-approved amendment to the constitution. The committee of 100, whose chairman was Waggoner Carr, also suggested higher ethical standards for lawmakers. Carr was speaker of the Texas House during the 1957 session when, in the wake of a bribery scandal involving a legislator, the current weak state ethics code was passed.

Mutscher and the team, however, figured that if both higher pay and higher ethical standards were needed, why not take the logical approach and combine the

*The outcome of that bit of appropriations chicanery: the appropriations conference committee contained $150,000 "for the removal of moss from the public waters of the state," with no limitation on where the moss-cutting would take place.

two? They did, and with disastrous results. The proposed constitutional amendment that emanated from that kind of team thinking would have created a legislative pay/state officials' ethics commission, empowered to recommend lawmakers' salaries, subject to approval by the House and Senate, and to establish and enforce ethical standards for all state employees. Led by Republican state chairman George Willeford of Austin, who called the amendment "pure political trickery," the voters overwhelmingly rejected the pay-ethics commission proposal. And since it was the first one on the ballot, its defeat may have helped drag down other amendments.*

Still the Mutscher group did not quit, determined as it was to prove by deeds that it was ethics-conscious after all. The House leadership next turned to a ten-year old ethics bill sponsored by Representative Jim Nugent of Kerrville, who also happened to be Mutscher's powerful chairman of the Rules committee. Mutscher self-consciously spurned any public role in the House's action, April 6, 7, and 13, 1971, on the ethics bill; he conveniently was in Washington, D.C., when the bill was brought to the House floor and debated the first two days. But he had left behind specific instructions not to allow the House to pass an ethics bill already approved by the Senate, a bill much stronger and broader than Nugent's original proposal. As might be expected, this stricter Senate bill did not pass. But even the devout Mutscher loyalists deserted on the main amendment to Nugent's ethics bill—a proposal by Representative Charles Patterson of Taylor to add an extensive

*The pay-ethics amendment was defeated, 505,620 to 274,780. Similarly, the voters vetoed by 428,009 to 346,165 an amendment that would have let the legislators propose constitutional amendments during special sessions as well as regular sessions. The welfare amendment, which would have allowed Texas a few more years' fiscal leeway in dealing with the welfare caseload increase, went down by 410,735 to 381,365. In fact, the only amendment that was approved had the effect of increasing from 5 per cent to 6 per cent the amount of interest paid on state-backed water-development bonds and authorizing $100 million in new sewage-treatment facility bonds; it was adopted by 410,868 to 365,553.

and revealing financial disclosure requirement. The Patterson amendment was adopted, 137 to 2, whereas a similar disclosure rule on January 20 had received only 24 favorable votes.

So, the Senate had passed an ethics bill that the House ignored; the House then passed an ethics bill that the Senate promptly ignored. It appeared for a while that the suddenly ethics-conscious Legislature actually might get through the session without having to do anything about the only aspect of the stock-fraud case that was clear to the public—the lack of strict, meaningful, enforceable ethical standards for state officials. The rhetoric about "ethics" had not died down, but the legislative process as it affected the ethics bill had atrophied.

Then Lieutenant Governor Ben Barnes, who at the time was basking in the sun of non-involvement in the stock-fraud case, stepped in to insist late in the session that an ethics bill of some sort be passed. The ensuing conference committee—with Senate conferees led by Senator Ralph Hall of Rockwall and House conferees by Representative Nugent*—lasted one week before a hastily written conference committee compromise ethics bill was sent to the House and the Senate at five minutes before midnight on May 31, 1971; that is to say, only five minutes before the session ended. The legislators did not have time to read the bill, of course, and probably no more than a dozen of the 181 members of the Legislature had any idea what the bill contained. But, in that kind of circumstance, it was a difficult political choice, and the bill passed the Senate with only five negative votes and the House with only six negative votes.**

The bill established a twelve-member ethics commission with statutory power, but with no staff, to investi-

*Other members of the ethics conference committee were Representatives Grant Jones of Abilene, Ace Pickens of Odessa, Jack Blanton of Carrollton, and Dean Cobb of Dumas, and Senators Charles Wilson of Lufkin, Pete Snelson of Midland, J. P. Word of Meridian, and Jack Hightower of Vernon.
**Senator Wayne Connally of Floresville, one of those voting against it, said he was opposed to an ethics bill "as a matter of principle."

gate alleged violations of a broad new list of ethical standards. Half of the ethics commission members were to be legislators, elected by their colleagues from the House and Senate. But the legislators would exercise a veto power given to no other group, because two members of the House serving on the commission could block an investigation of any House member and two senators on the commission could do the same for any of their colleagues. The financial disclosure provision was unnecessarily broad in its scope, covering not only all elected state officials, but also all appointed (even if unpaid) state officials, all state and local government employees earning more than $11,000 a year, all elected local officials (even if unpaid), and all candidates for public office.* There was some question, from the beginning, about how effective the legislature's financial disclosure provision would be. It required only the disclosure of soures of income—not amounts—and the lising of various financial and real estate transactions, without specific details that might reveal potential conflicts of interest.

As great as had been the public's demand for a strong new ethics law, however, prominent state officials wasted relatively little time in criticizing what the Legislature had produced. Specific and sometimes detailed criticisms of the law were issued in the fall of 1971 by Governor Smith, Secretary of State Bob Bullock, Supreme Court Chief Justice Robert W. Calvert, Court of Criminal Appeals Presiding Judge John Onion, Jr., and, oddly enough, Attorney General Crawford Martin. Martin's personal critique of the bill was odd in the sense that, as the state's chief lawyer, he would have been obligated to defend the ethics law if it had been taken

*Candidates for public office were added to the ethics bill's coverage during the special session that began immediately after the end of the regular session on May 31 and continued through June 4, 1971. Governor Smith refused to let the general subject of the ethics law be considered at the special session. But when no member of the House or Senate raised a constitutional point of order that the addition of candidates to the ethics bill was not included in the governor's "call" for the special session, Smith also did not object and allowed the bill to become law as amended.

to court. That was a fact he recognized implicitly when he said in his November 2, 1971, press release, "I would anticipate that the act will be taken to court in the near future by one or more political subdivisions to determine with finality if all of its provisions are constitutional." Martin then proceeded to outline how an effective legal attack could be made on the bill that he would be defending in court.

Fortunately for Martin, because it probably saved him some embarrassment, the ethics law never went to court. On January 6, 1972, in response to requests for opinions by Secretary of State Bullock and others, Martin declared the ethics bill "unconstitutional in its entirety." He cited as reasons the fact that the caption, or title, of the bill did not contain a reference to the financial disclosure provision; the fact that the California Supreme Court in 1970 declared a similarly broad financial disclosure provision to be unconstitutional because it did not deal precisely with conflict-of-interest situations; the fact that only two legislators serving on the twelve-member ethics commission would be able to prevent an investigation of a fellow legislator; and the assertion that the penal provisions of the new ethics law violated existing penal statutes.

Thus it was that on January 7, 1972, the voters of Texas found themselves in precisely the same position they were in on January 19, 1971, the day after the stock-fraud case was filed in Dallas: despite nearly a year-long demand for a new ethical climate in state government, Texas still had on the books only a vaguely worded 15-year-old ethics law that had never been enforced. And if it had been Mutscher who symbolized in the minds of many the need for a new state ethics law, it also was Mutscher who shouldered much of the blame for the law that the attorney general declared unconstitutional. For if Mutscher had not insisted that the Mutscher-dominated House reject the Senate-passed ethics bill half-way through the session, a new ethics law would have been in effect by mid-summer. Once more, however, the ethics hassle was a tribute of sorts to Mutscher's strength as a leader of the House, for his making the "team" stick together and "the system" work as long as it did.

In the process, some good legislation was passed—legislation, among other things, that likely will prevent a repetition of the banking and insurance scandals which in 1971 rocked the Texas political boat down to its ballast. But Mutscher's role was entirely passive as the Legislature enacted, almost exclusively at the initiative of a Senate special investigating committee, a complex package of banking and insurance reforms that gave state regulatory officials greater powers to deal with the kind of manipulations Frank Sharp used in the operation of Sharpstown State Bank and National Bankers Life Insurance Company. Among other things, the laws gave the Banking Department the power to remove officers and even to assume actual day-to-day operation of wayward banks and allowed the Insurance Department to prohibit insurance company take-overs that might be harmful to policyholders.

CHAPTER
TEN

The Most Undeliberate Body

In the east wing of the Capitol on the second floor, the Senate Chamber is an impressive majestic room. On a green-carpeted floor, partially surrounded by a highly polished brass rail, thirty-one handsome cherry-wood desks, spaciously allotted in four rows, face the dais and chair of the lieutenant governor. On the back wall two magnificent battle paintings—of the Alamo and San Jacinto—dominate the scene, providing an inspirational setting for the business at hand, while decorously spaced along the front and side, handsome portraits of such famous Texans as Stephen F. Austin and Lyndon B. Johnson adorn the walls. Even the senators have been somewhat awed by this setting, for as Oscar Mauzy of Dallas somberly reflected: "As one walks into this chamber, he is immediately struck by the feeling of history, by those events which have transpired, and which are our heritage."

Since 1888 a small group of men have helped shape the destiny of their fellow citizens in this quiet, elegant setting. And therefore in many ways they have tried to emulate the United States Senate, which is often called "the most deliberative body in the world." No doubt about it, the senators of the Sixty-second Legislature were—in comparison to the House—a more exclusive group in regard to numbers (thirty-one), experience, and power. Ranging in age from sixty-five (A.M. Aiken, Jr., of Paris) to thirty-four (Barbara Jordan of Houston), they were an older body, their average age being forty-five. A disproportionate number were lawyers (twenty)

and men (thirty). And most of them had served previously in some position of public trust. Because of
their limited number, they also developed a certain
camaraderie, a club-like atmosphere, in which the members, regardless of their political philosophies, were
quite protective of one another. [For instance, they
refused to pass the House Congressional redistricting
bill partly because Representative Clyde Haynes of
Vidor would have had a territorial advantage over
Senator Charles Wilson of Lufkin.]

Over the years the senators have developed and observed a number of unwritten rules which have also
preserved this camaraderie. Most fundamentally, they
do not lie to one another or, as one senator laughingly
commented, "You don't get caught lying." For if one
of them reneges on a vote after giving his word, his
influence thereafter is zero, the other members having
little more to do with him. Nor do they embarrass a
colleague by criticizing him before his constituents.
During the ethics bill and the corporate-profits tax bill
debates charges of "liar" arose, but such accusations
have been infrequent. Usually the comments are: "I believe that the senator has forgotten" or "the senator
will surely recollect." In other words, they may ac-
cuse each other privately of all sorts of foul motives and
deeds, but they try to maintain the personal integrity
of each member publicly since a loss of group prestige
might occur. In turn, they never try to hurt a colleague
at home, no matter how flagrant the indiscretion or how
much the personal dislike. And in regard to political
enemies, they respect the wishes of the senator personally involved. In executive session, for example,
when a senator states that a man from his district
whom the governor has appointed to some board or
commission is "personally obnoxious" to him, the
members vote to "bust"—reject—the nominee. This is
nearly always done unanimously.

Despite such attempts at exclusiveness and emula-
tion, the Texas Senate in comparison with its federal
counterpart is a most undeliberative body. And no
wonder! Both its rules (or lack of them) and precedents

have been obvious deterrents, allowing the senators little time to deliberate. Within 140 calendar days they must conduct state business for a two-year period, examining and judging as many as 4,500 pieces of legislation; yet following another unwritten rule, they seldom work more than a four-day week during the first three months of a session.* Consequently they do not have time to read all bills, to understand fully subsequent amendments, much less to debate openly the merits and weaknesses of the different measures.

With twenty-seven standing committees in the Senate, a senator has five, sometimes even ten or twelve committee assignments. For example, on some days Senator Mauzy had as many as three committee hearings scheduled at the same hour. Nor was this situation uncommon for many of the other senators. For the sake of expediency, they frequently resort to "floor-reporting" House measures — a technique by which a committee approves a bill without a public hearing or any rational discussion. Then, by a motion to suspend the rules (a two-thirds majority or twenty-one votes), they pass the bills through the constitutionally required second and third readings within several minutes. In fact during the 1969 special session, House bills 72 and 73, the Frank Sharp bank-deposit insurance bills, went through the Senate in this manner.

Equally damning to the Senate's status as a deliberative body has been its failure to keep minutes or records of its work and build an archives. In 1967 the senators did not even transcribe who voted for a bill in or out of committee, and not until 1971 did some committee chairmen tape-record their hearings; however, there has never been any rule forcing them to do so. Hence, new senators have never been able to orient themselves to what has previously taken place or to read the committee testimony of experts regarding the merits and defects of proposed legislation. Nor have

*Some political cynics have asserted, however, that the safest time for the people when the Legislature is in regular session is the weekend. With the representatives at home, the people cannot get hurt.

the courts, when the constitutionality of a measure has been challenged, had any evidence as to the legislators' intent. This lack of a complete, permanent legislative record also contributed to the strength of lobbying groups over the years.

Probably most responsible for the Senates' undeliberativeness, however, have been special-interest groups that learned the rules of the game and then used them to advantage. Of course, lobbyists have invariably provided legitimate, helpful services to legislators, furnishing them with information and thereby giving one side of an issue fully. But in the Texas Senate—and also in the House—they have affected legislation out of proportion to their numbers and clients.

In the action-packed Sixty-second Legislature, the lobbyists had a special advantage—the lack of time for thought about legislation. With senators so hard-pressed for time, the lobbyists had an edge in committee hearings. By concentrating on one or two important measures, while the legislator was rushing to several hearings, they were able to mobilize their forces. At times they had the majority vote; but, if in the minority, they used other political techniques. At times they or their agents "chubbed"* a bill to death or lined up witnesses ad infinitum to exhaust the opposition, or broke a quorum by having "their" senators stay away from the hearing. Equally effective was the traditional Senate practice of requiring suspension of the rules (by a two-thirds majority) in order to consider a bill out of its regular calendar order. Hence, the senators could by-pass and delay the vote on a critical or controversial measure indefinitely.** But if necessary, when all else failed, many lobbyists resorted to threats—veiled or direct—but more often to money. "Sure, it's common knowledge; we all gossip about it," one senator candidly stated to the authors in a tape-recorded interview in regard to lobbyists slipping cash to some legislators. In fact, he related, one colleague's favorite comment is: "The best

**The abortion bill fell victim to this technique.
*To "chub" means to delay and stall.

day in the world is just before a vote: you get paid $1,000 to vote the way you're already committed to vote anyway." And since a conference committee (five senators and five representatives) could decide the fate of a bill, some members found their positions economically advantageous.

But what made this exclusive club of 1971 so unique was its make-up. With only thirty-one politicians to claim the spotlight the individual members became, as they often referred to themselves, "thirty-one prima donnas," although having the same frailties and strengths as their fellowmen. Consequently the pressures of this short regular session—the long hours of work and play, the endless free feeds and booze parties, the ubiquitous lobbyists and home-town constituents plying their cause, the temptations presented by pretty and oftentimes aggressive young women—magnified their strengths, played upon their weaknesses, and taxed their physical and mental stamina. Then with the stock-fraud scandal ever-present after the first week of the session, with everyone trying to stay clear of the "big smear" but realizing that they were receiving strokes from the same brush, the senators became even more tense and nervous. As the session continued, several appeared on the Senate floor highly inebriated; two carried pistols (one had a shoulder holster and the other used his belt); while one collected the damnedest assortment of beauties — admiringly called "The Harem"—ever assembled in one office. In fact, this senator was reportedly complaining at times because none of his girls could type and get his work out.

Yet the caliber of certain senators was surprisingly high, considering the fact that the $400 per month remuneration was insufficient and bordering on the ridiculous. As criteria for leadership and power, a point system would have to include such important considerations as seniority and experience, brainpower and industry, service on committees, friendship with the lieutenant governor, and the senator's role in the Sixty-second Legislature. For instance, Jim Wallace of Houston and Max Sherman of Amarillo were particularly outstanding as freshman senators but, as both admitted, this session was a learning experience for them, a preparation for future service, a foundation for more effective representation.

Among the many senators interviewed, A. M. Aiken, Jr., of Paris was always the first name mentioned. As chairman of the Finance committee and a member of the Education committee, he was automatically in a powerful position; however, there were other significant considerations. Having been in the Senate since 1937—more than a year before Ben Barnes was born— "the Dean" was in effect the majority leader for the lieutenant governor. Because of his knowledge of state government and of parliamentary procedure, he was highly respected. Always a man of his word, hardworking and conscientious, he nevertheless received occasional criticism for being old-fashioned, a traditionalist who sincerely loved the Senate but who had not changed his philosophy in the last thirty-four years. Yet in his calm, quiet way he had a sobering effect upon the senators whenever tempers verged upon explosion.

Directly across the aisle from Aiken on the first row sat William Tyler (Bill) Moore of Bryan, a powerfully-built man in his early fifties, somewhat distinguished-looking with graying hair. As chairman of the State Affairs committee and actually the floor leader for the lieutenant governor, "The Bull of the Brazos"—he has been known to bellow during his twenty-two years of service—was second only to Barnes in regard to "raw power." Smart, witty, and tough, he was the most feared man in the Senate, a person no one wanted to pick a fight with, or to have as an enemy; for if you "crossed him," one colleague commented, "look out. He is totally independent, totally pragmatic, and . . . mean as hell." For example, he thoroughly detested Joe Bernal of San Antonio and told him so quite expressively. Then from the beginning of the 1971 session he openly opposed Lufkin Senator Charles Wilson's public utilities commission bill and, through experience and knowledge of parliamentary maneuvering, was largely responsible for killing it. Even those colleagues who disagreed with his rural-oriented conservative philosophy respected him, for as one of them grudgingly admitted: "Bill Moore is one of the most entertaining and delightful people I know if you just realize the fact that he is the prototype of the old southern cracker-barrel politician."

On the front row also was J. P. Word of Meridian, the lieutenant governor's closest friend. Concerning their relationship, Robert Spellings stated: "Barnes would trust Word with his life and Word is worthy of that trust." And for that reason, if for no other, "Big Word" who is 6'4" and 250 pounds, had tremendous political swat because his comments usually reflected those of Barnes. But being the chairman of the all-important Redistricting committee and a member of the five-man budget-writing Finance subcommittee made him even more influential. Yet he did not abuse his power, although a product of a rural society in an increasingly urban and liberal body.

Not as prominent as Aiken, Moore, and Word but surely important in the Sixty-second Legislature was Tom Creighton of Mineral Wells.* Nicknamed "Tom the Tax Man" by political opponent Walt Steimel of Fort Worth for advocating a broader-based sales tax (including food and medicine) in the 1969 session, he was the chief representative of the business community. Probably the most conservative member of the Senate philosophically—even more than Republican Henry Grover of Houston, who was nicknamed "the Nazi"—Creighton logically was chosen to carry the ball against the corporate profits tax measure. Although at times trying to appear "folksy" and "country" or, as one close friend suggested, "a Jaycee who has never grown up," he was actually putting on an act. For "Uncle Tom," as he was also called, is a capable attorney, a suave, charming man who has seldom been on the

*In 1970 Barnes campaigned for and helped elect Creighton in District 22, thus assuring continued support from his good friend.

losing side. And as a member of the Finance subcommittee, he made sure of it.

In opposition to the conservatives was Oscar Mauzy of Dallas, recognized by most of the press, the conservative senators, and political observers as the leader of the liberal group in the Senate or, as they called themselves, "the Good Guys."* Highly articulate and cogent in his arguments—and seemingly even more so before an audience—he became the favorite of the Capitol correspondents, an extremely quotable person whom the young idealistic legislative aides and office workers idolized. For, to them, he advocated necessary reform legislation and was disliked by all the right people—Mutscher and Heatly, the insurance lobby, and the so-called business hierarchy in Dallas. Sometimes called "the dealer" by his colleagues, he preferred to work behind the scenes, to organize the liberal senators, and to plan both offensive and defensive strategy. Unwisely, however, he spread himself too thin, sponsoring over a hundred bills during the session. At times he also became too impatient with obtuseness, with obvious ploys of deceit, and would lash out at the opposition. Yet, because of his close friendship with Barnes, and more importantly because of his tremendous industry and ability, he was able to push legislation through the Senate concerning the jury wheel, comparative negligence, group automobile insurance, and prohibitive child abuse.

Equally personable but less controversial, Joe Christie of El Paso came into prominence for advocating a tough liquor-by-the-drink law. A man who always did his homework, who was good at counting votes, he was also a member of the important Finance subcommittee. But after the passage of liquor-by-the-drink early in the session, "José" (so nicknamed because he is bilingual and from El Paso) faded from the limelight. He nevertheless was a steadying force in the Senate,

---

*"The Good Guys," however, claimed that no one spoke for them, that all were chiefs and none were Indians. They therefore personified the cliche of divide and conquer.

reliable and unabrasive, a man who would not succumb to pressure.

The mouthpiece for the "Good Guys" was A. R. "Babe" Schwartz of Galveston, who "was vaccinated," a friend laughed, "with a phonograph needle." Elected to the Senate in 1961, when liberals were scarce, he became the loyal opposition, providing a kind of negative leadership. Hence for years he fought unavailingly against turned-off, tuned-out colleagues, haranguing and chastising them for what he considered to be their blindness. In fact, the usual comment of his opponents was "he's got more guts than brains." A knowledgeable lawyer and senator, especially regarding appropriations, he was appointed by Barnes, to the horror of many conservatives, to the Finance subcommittee.

Also in the leadership of the "Good Guys" was Don Kennard of Fort Worth, sometimes known as the "Happy Whale" or "Senators"—could just one man be that big? A veteran legislator for twenty years, he seemed at the first of the 1971 session to have lost his drive and enthusiasm. After about five weeks, however, he became a transformed man, casting aside his lethargy and utilizing his experience and ability for a great personal triumph. "That damn Kennard is insufferable to live with," Mauzy admiringly commented late in March. "He's trying to work us all to death." Consequently Barnes decided to give him more important responsibilities other than his committee assignments on State Affairs and Jurisprudence. After Charles Wilson declined the sponsorship of the consumer-laden tax bill proposed by the Senate, Barnes offered the job to Kennard. Although realizing the political pitfalls of such an assignment, the Happy Whale—who dieted off forty-five pounds in eight weeks—accepted the assignment, succinctly reasoning that "somebody had to." But actually his big moment of stamina and determination came near the end of the session when he filibustered to death Rockwall Senator Ralph Hall's proposed four-year school for the University of Texas at Dallas. Almost without anyone's help, Kennard stood before his desk and talked for twenty-nine hours and twenty-two minutes, unwilling even then to relinquish the floor until the opposition conceded defeat.

Besides these senators several others made their presence felt. Jack Hightower of Vernon, sometimes called the Billy Graham of the Senate, was president pro tem during the session. A compassionate, considerate man, highly respected by his colleagues, he usually received such touchy peacemaker jobs as chairman of the Administration committee, which designated office space and additional funds to the "prima donnas." Considered also as one of the most able senators in terms of ability and intelligence was Charles Herring of Austin. Sometimes called "The Fox," he was chairman of the Jurisprudence committee which screened important bills having to do with the penal code, drugs, and liquor. In fact, his committee amended the liquor-by-the-drink bill into its present form. And then in regard to sheer brainpower and articulate leadership, Barbara Jordan of Houston was near the top of the list with almost every senator. Yet, obviously quite concerned about Congressional redistricting, she did not assert herself as much as she had in the 1969 session.

Regardless of such individual leadership and despite the fact that the "Good Guys" supposedly had a seventeen to fourteen voting advantage, Ben Barnes was the all-pervasive and dominating force in the Senate, setting the legislative pace and controlling each day's play. From the lieutenant governor all powers, and therefore all blessings, flowed—and the senators knew it. After all, he appointed the chairman of every committee, which usually obligated those favored senators to him. But if need be, he could hold them in line because of his power to refer bills to committees. With such authority he could make any committee prominent or insignificant. For that matter, if he had followed Mutscher's example of punishing his opposition, he could have kept bills from being considered altogether. Barnes, however, was too smart a politician to fall into that trap, to lay himself open to charges of a dictatorship and oppressiveness; there was no need to do so. He had men whom he had campaigned for, who were personal friends, who owed him favors, who (like Aiken) were loyal to the Chair. And by giving every one "a run" at legislation (if they could get twenty-one votes), by appearing to be fair and impartial, he won their admiration and respect.

At the same time, however, Barnes held some cudgels over the senators' heads. They could never be sure that he might not be vindictive, that he might not "gut" their bills and try to destroy them politically. In the 1971 session especially, Barnes had incredibly powerful levers for control. Almost all the senators were concerned about senatorial redistricting which directly affected them. He could, conceivably, with the help of J. P. Word who was committee chairman, pit two men against each other or cut away their power base by placing certain supportive precincts or counties in another district. A few other senators, such as Barbara Jordan of Houston, Mike McKool of Dallas, Charles Wilson of Lufkin, and Murray Watson of Waco, were mightily concerned about congressional redistricting; hence Barnes could conceivably sway them to his way of thinking. And, of course, concerning appropriations, any senator was vulnerable to charges of ineffectiveness if certain projects in his district went unfunded. For instance, Joe Bernal of San Antonio and Ronald Bridges of Corpus Christi, both in the "Good Guys" camp, were quite nervous about adequate appropriations for their home-area universities. Consequently, Barnes held all these critical measures in abeyance until the last week of the session—and thus easily controlled.*

Nowhere was there better proof of Barnes' complete domination of the Senate than in the fight over the tax bill. As early as January 21, 1971, the liberals, nearly always having thirteen or fourteen of the seventeen senators in attendance, began meeting to discuss weekly as well as long-term strategy. By February 1,

*Because of a number of filibusters and unforeseen delays over appropriations, and the House-Senate fight over the Congressional redistricting bill, Barnes—much to his chagrin—was unable to pass a Senate redistricting bill.

Mauzy, Schwartz, and Wilson had obtained an office for two University of Texas law students (Terry O'Rourke and Griffith Smith) to research "various untapped tax sources." In turn, they invited experts on finance, including several University of Texas professors, to enlighten the weekly caucus on all aspects of taxation. And by the end of March they knew exactly how they wanted to raise adequate revenue for the state. Specifically, they advocated a corporate profits tax of 5 per cent (equal to the proposed state sales tax) which would raise approximately half a billion dollars each biennium. Altogether, they estimated a revenue package of $822,286,909 which would more than meet all state fiscal responsibilities.* With supposedly seventeen votes of "Good Guys" in the Senate, they were girding themselves to win an unprecedented and hard-fought battle against the conservatives.

But Barnes was not about to let a corporate profits tax pass the Senate. Besides having little or no chance to be accepted by the more conservative House of Representatives, it violated one of Barnes' rules—for surely it would disturb his money base. After persuading Kennard to "carry" the tax measure, he depended on the wily and experienced Bill Moore, as chairman of the State Affairs committee, to hammer out a measure upon which a majority (sixteen) of the senators could agree. After two weeks of open public hearings during April, Moore had a tax package which would meet the fiscal needs of the state and which had a chance, he believed, to pass both the House and the Senate. So on Monday morning, April 26, at the invitation of Barnes, the State Affairs subcommittee breakfasted at the lieutenant governor's apartment where, by a four to three vote, the members adopted a report raising the general sales tax from 3.25 to 4 per cent (an estimated $298,-550,000), taxing sales and rental of automobiles at 4 per cent ($79,400,000), increasing the franchise tax ($102,-

*See the sixty-two page report entitled "A Consumer Viewpoint on State Taxation: An Analysis of Alternative Tax Proposals for the 62nd Legislature," March 31, 1971, which Mauzy and Schwartz published and distributed.

650,000), and adding three cents per package to cigarettes and two cents a gallon to gas ($148,800,000).[1] Then that afternoon the full State Affairs committee considered and easily adopted it in toto, together with an amendment by Charles Wilson which increased the beer tax from $3.40 to $6.00 a barrel ($28,800,000),[2] whereupon Moore stated that the committee recommendations would be printed on Tuesday and on every senator's desk by Wednesday morning ready for immediate consideration.

On April 28, in an intensely emotional atmosphere, the vital issue came up for a vote, and the Senate voted down the corporate profits tax by a 16 to 15 vote.[3] This vote took the heart out of the liberals. After April 28 they seemed to have lost their organization, their spirit, their will to fight. For many of them, like Schwartz and Mauzy, the session was virtually over, although more than a month still remained. They all watched with interest and concern the unfolding developments in the stock-fraud scandal. But the members were even more interested in trying to salvage whatever political plums possible. Nearly all were concerned about senatorial redistricting; a few were specifically interested in carving out favorable congressional districts for themselves, while all wanted to pass specific bills and receive substantial appropriations for their districts. Now only one man could grant their wishes—the unquestionable leader of the Senate, Ben Barnes.

Towards the end of May, emotions rose as the session neared its close. The Capitol became a madhouse on May 31; at midnight the regular session would be over. In the House, sleepless representatives leveled bitter tirades and invectives at one another, letting loose

[1]Moore, Creighton, Ike Harris of Dallas, and Doc Blanchard of Lubbock voted for the measure while Kennard, Herring, and Jordan opposed it. In all, the tax package was estimated at a little more than $629,000,000.

[2]Wilson originally had recommended a tax of $10.00 a barrel.

[3]Rumors were spread that 300 businessmen had agreed to put $2,000 each into a kitty to fight re-election of any senator who voted for the corporate profits tax.

pent-up emotions against Gus Mutscher who had at last lost control. The appropriations, tax, and redistricting bills—three levers enabling discipline and control—had now passed and many members were furious, even outraged, upon seeing the speaker blatantly seek to eliminate, "to take care of," at least half of his most outspoken enemies. "It's a real show, a Roman circus," Garland and Lois Ham of Arlington exclaimed. "It's quite a spectacle." And it was. State gladiators were in deadly verbal combat, trying to destroy one another by laying the groundwork for the 1972 campaign, by pointing out to the voters who the Mutscher men were.

In the Senate the situation was not much better. The "thirty-one prima donnas" were tired and worn, the strain of 140 strenuous days of in-fighting and frustration obviously apparent. They were unhappy with the performance of the state representatives, with their petty games and shabby maneuverings. They definitely did not appreciate earlier attempts by the House to make them look bad before the public by passing a totally inadequate tax bill, thereby forcing the Senate to add even more taxes. Nor did the senators like the infuriating House strategy of substituting House bills for Senate-passed measures, simply because the representatives wanted to bolster their record with legislation carrying their name. But even more frustrating, they knew that the House could not unclog its calendar in these last few hours; therefore, hundreds of their bills would die without a final vote. So for the moment they were unwilling to contest the comment that the west wing of the Capitol (the House side) should be called the National Bankers Life wing.

Yet most of the senators were aggravated, if not disgusted, with the legislative process *per se*. Although having worked extremely long hours, what had they accomplished—at least in a calm, deliberative way? Almost half the legislation had been pushed through in the last two weeks. Nearing the completion of his first term, Senator Jim Wallace of Houston was appalled at some of the things that he had witnessed—

the glaring injustice of floor-reporting a bill, the gross ineptness caused by receiving a 400-page appropriations conference report only seventy-two hours before the end of the session, the unbelievable pressure and rush of the last few days during which no senator could possibly be cognizant of more than a small percentage of what was happening. Equally concerned, Senator Joe Christie pointed to the committee system as a basic area needing reform. But even more revealing was his experience with the conference committee on appropriations where a few men, like Heatly, added over $65 million of the taxpayers' money to a measure that could only be voted up or down with no amendments or discussion. In fact, at this late date all the senators realized that there was no time, by the present rules of the game, to know much about what they were voting on, much less to pass legislation that affected them directly; for it was becoming increasingly apparent that they could not pass a Senate redistricting bill by midnight.

Their anger and frustrations, however, were nothing compared to that of the non-professionals, those people who watched the legislative process closely but did not work within it. For four months many of them had expected some kind of action which would restore faith in state government. Not realizing, like most people, that Mutscher had lost control of the House, Frank Inman of the UAW was outraged that the legislators had seemingly condoned such activities. "How much farther down are we gonna have to scrape to get to the bottom?" he and another labor leader asked: "If an incident like this had happened in a UAW local union, the officer would have immediately been suspended until it was thoroughly investigated. But here we've gone through 140 days of the Texas Legislature and neither the Speaker nor the Governor has as yet come forward and explained to the people what has happened." To the surprise and chagrin of most Texans, it seemed that the legislative and executive branches had acquired lockjaw and paralysis.

Despite widespread disillusionment there were certain pockets of hope, of positive reaction, around the Capitol. In Don Kennard's office, legislative aide Tom Schieffer of Fort Worth felt that in the long run the scandal could be beneficial, for the "people might wake up in Texas and see what was going on . . . and not put up with it any more." He therefore decided to run for office and, if elected, try to help "change the whole atmosphere in Austin."

In Senator Ron Bridges' office Sue Lowe of Austin, Bill Harrison and Bob Thorpe of Corpus Christi, reflected much the same attitude. At first they were disappointed, Bob Thorpe recollected, with the "very poor way" of running state government, with the fantastic "pork barrel," with representatives "grabbing" political plums for themselves and their districts instead of doing what was best for Texas overall. "Yes, we've talked about this, the legislative process and the events of the last few months," Sue Lowe concluded. "And I think that the three of us agree that this has made us more determined to do something to change it."

CHAPTER
ELEVEN

The Body Count Is Rising

Speaker Gus Mutscher's political career was over, essentially, on the night of May 31, 1971. That was the final day of the regular session of the Sixty-second Legislature, and by the stroke of midnight a majority of the incumbent House members were pledged, either publicly or privately, *not* to support Mutscher for another term as speaker.

Many of the Mutscher defectors had made their pledges privately earlier in the session but had stayed on the team publicly, they explained, in order to keep alive the hope of passing additional legislation important to them personally or politically. Mutscher's floor leaders had put out the word that there was to be no public ship-jumping at least until the tax, appropriations, and redistricting bills were passed; the implied threat was that a deserter, caught in the act, would not be allowed to pass any more of his bills.

"Mutscher just got to be too much for us," said Representative William O. Braecklein of Dallas in a comment typical of those who had served Mutscher loyally for two sessions but who could do so no longer. Braecklein, who at one point was Mutscher's main line of contact with the cohesive and potent Dallas County delegation, was one of the many conscientious conservatives who had simply had enough of the speaker's methods of control. He elaborated on his revulsion with Mutscher, noting it was caused as much by the speaker's way of doing things as by the speaker's involvement in the stock-fraud case.

But Braecklein and other former Mutscher loyalists were set apart from later defectors in a key way—the

difference being *when* they split off from the team. The
Braecklein group defected at the end of the spring legislative session. The later defectors, including such team
stalwarts as Representatives Joe Golman of Dallas and
Harold Davis of Austin, did not leave the speaker's
camp until September 23, 1971, or later—after Mutscher, Shannon, and McGinty had been indicted and
after Mutscher's demise had been assured. And a month
after the indictments, a clear majority of House members not only opposed Mutscher's re-election as speaker
but, according to a United Press International poll,
thought Mutscher should resign immediately as speaker.

Mutscher's troubles were not over, however. Later
investigations revealed that Mutscher and some of his
political allies, chiefly McGinty, had been trying to use
their positions of public office to enrich themselves in
other ways.* Mutscher continued to be plagued, too, by
the fact that Frank Sharp, who was granted immunity
from further prosecution in exchange for his cooperation with investigators, spent much of the summer and
fall of 1971 traveling around Texas to testify about the
stock-fraud case.

Mutscher's own problems also were transmogrified
into political problems for many of the House members
who had supported him. In the leadership vacuum
created by the decline of the speaker, about forty-five of
the still-loyal Mutscherites held a series of meetings to
choose a candidate to succeed Mutscher. On October
24, 1971, at a session in San Antonio, the list was nar-

*The speaker's own financial problems were acute. In addition
to being a defendant in civil actions seeking damages because
of the stock-fraud case, Mutscher also was sued August 12, 1971,
by the Federal Deposit Insurance Corp. for payment of a $332,008
loan from Sharpstown State Bank to buy a second block of
National Bankers Life stock. According to later investigations,
Mutscher and McGinty also sought financial aid from other
interest groups—including W. L. Moody and Sons Bankers (Unincorporated), a private bank in Galveston whose owner, Shearn
Moody, Jr., sought and obtained passage of legislation in 1971
permitting the state of Texas to deposit state funds in private
banks. It did not help the speaker's cause any, either, for Mutscher to excuse his financial hustling on the ground that he
needed an airplane and traveling money in order to be "more
independent" of the business lobby.

rowed to Representatives Dean Cobb of Dumas, Dave Finney of Fort Worth, Jim Nugent of Kerrville, Joe Salem of Corpus Christi, Jim Slider of Naples, and John Traeger of Seguin. Nugent, a twelve-year veteran of the House and chairman of the Rules committee. emerged as the consensus candidate of the remaining members of the Mutscher team. But even Nugent, regarded as a maverick and occasionally as a heretic by the conventional-wisdom forces, found that his in-House reputation of forceful independence could not completely overcome his public image as a Mutscher team tool. This became all the more obvious when session-ending speeches critical of Mutscher were purged from the House Journal, mysteriously and inexplicably, by the censorship process under Nugent's direction in his position as chairman of the Rules committee.

Nugent was not the only speaker candidate suffering from the Mutscher syndrome. Representative Rayford Price of Palestine, considered the early front-running speaker candidate, was tagged by his opponents as a Mutscher man—despite the fact that Price had broken with Mutscher publicly immediately after the start of the 1971 legislative session. But Representative Fred Head, a moderate member of the Dirty 30, moved from Henderson back to his home town of Troup in order to run against Price because, Head said, Price "was always counted on the other [Mutscher] side."

The Mutscher "slop-over," as some Capitol newsmen called it, extended beyond the speakership race. All over the state, starting in the early summer of 1971, eight months before the filing deadline, candidates began announcing against incumbent legislators who had been loyal to Mutscher. The pace picked up when the speaker refused to step down after he was indicted—a refusal that delighted his opponents, who were eager to use Mutscher as an election-year issue. Most of the anti-incumbent candidates were young professional men campaigning on reform platforms seeking an end to "Mutscherism" in the Texas House of Representatives. Thanks largely to Mutscher, then, the 1972 party primaries included more contested legislative races, offered a better grade of candidates, and presented a wider choice to the public than at any time in recent history.

Mutscher was not the only Texas politician suffering from the fallout of the stock-fraud case. He was merely the most prominent and the most severely wounded. Governor Preston Smith and Dr. Elmer Baum did not win any public prizes for their involvement in the allegations, despite the governor's having vetoed the bank-deposit insurance bills. Baum was forced to resign his position on the state banking board when it became obvious in the spring of 1971 that the Senate would not confirm his nomination. (He had been serving without confirmation since September 11, 1969.) In October, 1971, Baum also resigned under fire as chairman of the State Democratic Executive Committee—a resignation that sparked a Democratic leadership fight in which Governor Smith was defeated in his attempt to enforce the tradition that an incumbent governor is entitled to his choice of state chairman. Mayor Roy Orr of De Soto, a conservative member of the SDEC, won the chairmanship on October 20 by two votes over Agriculture Commissioner John C. White, a liberal who was Smith's candidate for that position. Smith's own fumbling of the chairmanship fight contributed to White's defeat, but there were undertones of resentment about the stock-fraud case among SDEC members who supported Orr. There was other evidence that the Smith-Baum involvement in the stock-fraud case hurt Democratic politicians—particularly in Democratic finance chairman French Robertson's statement that contributions to the party declined after the SEC case was filed.

Smith also was being criticized in late 1971 and early 1972 for something entirely unrelated to the stock-fraud case—his appointments to the new nine-member Texas Vending Commission, a regulatory agency whose creation in 1971 followed by two years a controversial industry-directed restructuring of the coin-operated amusements industry.* Governor Smith in September, 1971, named as chairman of the commission Raymond B. Williams of Dallas, one of the Texas vending industry's

*For a brief discussion of the vending industry laws in the context of legislative reform, see the following chapter.

biggest operators and a contributor of $5,000 to Smith's 1970 campaign. Smith also named two other industry men to the commission, and two "public" members of the commission appointed by Smith had business relations with the industry. The result was that Smith's appointments gave the vending industry a sympathetic majority of the commission. And although it seemed clear that the vending commission appointments were not connected to the stock-fraud case, most observers agreed that the stock scandals made all public officials more vulnerable to conflict-of-interest charges.

It was no great surprise, therefore, that shortly after Smith announced on November 19, 1971, that he would seek a third term as governor, The Texas Poll showed Smith at an all-time low in popularity with Texans over eighteen years of age. Joe Belden of Dallas, director of the poll, said only 33 per cent of Texans approved of Smith's performance as governor while 54 per cent disapproved—down from 37 per cent approval and 48 per cent disapproval in March, 1971, and far below Smith's rating of 56 per cent approval and only 25 per cent disapproval in June, 1970.

But if Smith had been statistically hurt by the scandal, Lieutenant Governor Ben Barnes felt personally hurt by it. Barnes felt he was wrongly accused every step of the way and he admitted the accusations affected his political standing, mostly because of the mere mention of his name in news stories about the scandal. Although he took an aggressive approach in responding to the accusations—for the most part criticizing Frank Sharp—Barnes still was harmed by the general climate of distrust in state government. The lieutenant governor was damaged further when it was discovered, early in November, 1971, that he was using state employees to produce a computerized mailing list of 90,000 names and addresses—ostensibly for mailing Christmas cards but potentially for soliciting campaign assistance. That was only a week after Barnes, using money from his benefactor Herman Bennett, paid off the remainder of the controversial $60,000 loan, originally from the Sharp empire's Dallas Bank and Trust Co.—the loan that constituted Barnes' closest connection to the stock-fraud case.*

Barnes, however, was not alone in tangential involvement in the stock-fraud scandal, for at least two other high-ranking state officials' names were brought into the public discussion. Treasurer Jesse James deposited more than $10 million in state funds in Sharpstown State Bank between 1968 and 1970—more than in any of the so-called non-district banks. Republican Representative Maurice Angly of Austin charged that James' deposit practices cost the state more than $1 million in additional revenue that could have been earned by investing the same money differently. At the same time, Angly revealed that the sale of James' lodges on Lake Travis to Houston interests was financed in part with $90,000 in loans from Sharpstown State Bank and National Bankers Life Insurance Co. James also had been a member of the state banking board when the charter for Sharpstown State Bank was approved. James' response was to fire Jim Hill (Angly's father-in-law) as head of the escheat division, to argue that state-held collateral prevented any loss in state funds from the collapse of the Sharpstown bank, and to say that he knew nothing about the financing of the sale of his Lake Travis Lodges.

Attorney General Crawford Martin, who already had played a minor role in investigation of the stock-fraud case, also got some free newspaper publicity when it was revealed in October, 1971, that he received a "stock tip" from Frank Sharp—while Martin and his family were Sharp's ranch guests late in 1969 and again at Sharp's Houston office early in 1970. Sharp was trying personally to sell National Bankers Life stock to Martin, although the attorney general said that Sharp never mentioned the possibility of Sharpstown Bank loans to buy the stock. Martin said that he turned the stock offer

*The loan was arranged by Barnes' executive assistant Robert Spellings and Harold Hinn, a prominent Dallas investor and long-time friend of Barnes. Barnes said he did not know until some four months later that the loan had been made, and was unaware until the SEC suit was filed that Dallas Bank and Trust Co. was controlled by Sharp interests.

down because it would have cost too much, because NBL was in "shaky" condition, and because he did not buy "speculative" stocks. He did not comment on the ethical aspects of a state official's accepting a stock tip of that sort—perhaps because Martin, as attorney general, had ruled in favor of Sharp on a key legal issue about Sharpstown State Bank only two and one-half years before Sharp made the stock offer to Martin. (Martin's ruling had the effect of increasing the bank's capitalization dramatically and thus its ability to make large loans, ultimately giving Sharp the financial resources he used in the manipulations charged by the SEC.) Martin, as attorney general, also had been put in charge of a 1971 investigation of the stock-fraud case.*

One of Martin's predecessors as attorney general, Will Wilson, lost his job as a result of the stock-fraud case. Wilson, who had served on the Texas Supreme Court and was elected to three terms as a self-styled "crime-busting" attorney general, became a stock-fraud casualty because of his close and profitable relationship with Frank Sharp. A Democrat until he lost races for the United States Senate in 1961 and for governor in 1962, Wilson entered private law practice in Austin and became a Republican. One of his more lucrative jobs was as general counsel for Frank Sharp at what the SEC said was the beginning of the stock-fraud scheme—the summer, 1968, purchase of National Bankers Life Insurance Co. from former Governor Allan Shivers, a $7.5 million purchase that Wilson negotiated for Sharp. NBL was paid for with money from other Sharp companies that had borrowed from Sharpstown State Bank—which Wilson had voted to charter when he was serving on the state banking board.

When President Richard Nixon took office, he called

---

*Martin was directed by a House resolution (which was approved by Speaker Mutscher) to head a panel of public and private citizens in an investigation. But the resolution was vague enough to render the study almost meaningless from the start, and some of the private citizens named to the panel—notably Morris Harrell of Dallas, president of the State Bar of Texas—refused to cooperate. Martin's first step in the investigation was to demand that the SEC produce whatever evidence it had to indicate that state officials were bribed.

Will Wilson away from the field of corporate law and put him in charge of the Justice Department's criminal division—as an assistant attorney general at a salary about one-third of what Wilson was making as a lawyer. Naturally when the stock-fraud case broke, Wilson was blamed by many Texas Democrats for the whole thing. He was, they said, the protagonist in a purely political purge. Just as naturally, Wilson announced that he had disqualified himself from the case entirely because of his previous business affiliation with Sharp.

Wilson resigned his position in the Nixon Administration on October 15, 1971, after three months of almost daily criticism from Congressman Henry B. Gonzalez of San Antonio. Gonzalez cited Wilson's legal service to Sharp in the context of the Justice Department's still-mysterious grant of immunity to Sharp in exchange for a guilty plea, a three-year suspended sentence, and a $5,000 fine on relatively minor charges. The sweeping, but not unprecedented, grant of immunity to Sharp meant that neither the federal government nor state agencies could prosecute him for anything other than contempt of court and perjury. But Gonzalez argued that the government did not get a bargain when it "bought" Sharp's cooperation because Sharp himself should have been sent to jail. He also accused the Justice Department of seeking immunity for Sharp in order to protect Wilson.

Wilson's resignation followed by seven weeks the publication of an unsworn statement detailing his professional and financial relationships with Sharp. That included borrowing more than a quarter of a million dollars from Sharp-controlled companies, and $30,000 on an unsecured loan in August, 1970, while Sharp already was under investigation by two federal agencies. Wilson also had paid, perhaps without knowing it, a $2,500 bill in 1967 for "bugging" rooms where federal bank examiners were studying the operations of Sharpstown State Bank. And he had allowed his brokerage account to be used for the purchase of 1,000 shares of NBL stock for federal bank examiner Ted Bristol and his wife; Wilson said that he did not ask about or know Bristol, who later was indicted because of the stock deal. (Wilson would have been subject to a criminal charge if he had known Bristol's position as a bank examiner.)

Wilson told President Nixon in his resignation letter that he was quitting to prevent further "difficulties" and "embarrassment" to the Nixon Administration. He also said, in what may have been an indication of his future course, "I must fight my own fight, freed from the restraints of this office."

With some irony, Wilson later charged he was forced out of his federal position by hold-over Democrats in the Nixon Administration's Justice Department. For when the SEC case was first filed, many of those named in the suit, including John Osorio and Waggoner Carr, claimed Wilson was behind it all. As the case developed, it must have occurred to Wilson, Osorio, and Carr that they were all in the same boat.

Osorio and Carr were almost wiped out by the stock-fraud case, economically and professionally. Osorio was indicted on several criminal charges and both Osorio and Carr were found guilty of securities violations in the SEC civil case in Dallas, although Carr appealed that decision. Civil damage suits were filed against Osorio, Carr, and most of the other principals in the scandal. And the Internal Revenue Service sought to collect $54,973 from Osorio in back taxes from his dealings with RIC International Industries, which was marginally involved in the stock-fraud case.

Carr probably also suffered a fatal blow politically. The day the stock-fraud case was filed, he was meeting with a group of long-time supporters to discuss the possibility of Carr's making a political comeback in 1972. He said "without a doubt" he would have made a 1972 race for lieutenant governor, governor, or senator if the stock-fraud case had not exploded in his face.

From the time the stock-fraud case was filed, then, the political body count kept rising. At one point, it even seemed possible that the scandal would reach to that paragon of Texas political success, former President Lyndon Johnson. But no connection between LBJ and the stock-fraud-related activities of his former aide Jake Jacobsen was ever developed.*

No one could be sure precisely how the scandals would affect Texas politics in the decade of the 1970's. Certainly the Republicans could take heart and be optimistic about their chances to convert Texas into a two-party state at last. But in the Democratic camp, analytical confusion reigned. SDEC chairman Roy Orr predicted "a few individuals who happen to be in the Democratic party" would be hurt by the scandal. But he added: "The Democratic party as a whole has been too good to the people of Texas for the people to give up the party. . . . The Democratic party has made Texas what it is today." Lieutenant Governor Barnes, on the other hand, said flatly: "I don't think there is any point in fooling ourselves about our present situation in the Texas Democratic party. We have cratered. But when you hit bottom, there is only one way to go and that's up." So there was no unanimity about the future course of the state, except the belief of most analysts that some measure of reform in the legislative process would result.

Then, symbolically, as the year of the stock-fraud scandal ended, the Securities and Exchange Commission quietly announced a promotion for Robert Watson, the hard-working and effective lawyer-investigator who had developed and tried the stock-fraud case in Dallas federal court.

*Jacobsen, who had been working for Texas politicians since Price Daniel's tenure as governor, and his law partner Joseph R. Long bought control of City Bank and Trust Co. of Dallas from the Frank Sharp interests shortly after the stock-fraud case was filed. At that time, Jacobsen said he and Long had "no connection with Frank Sharp, the Sharpstown State Bank, or any others named in the recent (SEC) litigation." Subsequent investigations, however, indicated that nearly a year earlier Jacobsen helped Sharp hire Dallas Albert Johnson as chief executive officer of the Sharpstown bank and that Jacobsen and an investment partner received nearly $4 million in loans from the Sharp-owned National Bankers Life Insurance Co. While Jacobsen and Long had been associated with former President Johnson in various ways, there was no indication that LBJ was involved in the stock-fraud case.

CHAPTER
TWELVE

If People Only Knew—and Cared

It came as no surprise to many Texans when in February, 1971, newspapers blared headlines to the effect that "Legislature Ranks 38th in Nation" and "Our Boys Are 12th from Last." The headlines came, after all, at a time when public confidence in state government seemed to be at an all-time low. Top state officials and political figures stood indicted, in the public eye, of gross ethical behavior, yet the Legislature was doing nothing to see what went on in the stock-fraud scandal and how to correct the situation.

Thus, the general response to the headlines was either "So what else is new?" or "They don't deserve that much credit." But there was substance behind the report quoted in the newspapers, for it represented the first comprehensive national comparative study, both qualitative and quantitative, of state legislatures and their ability to perform effectviely. The study was made by the Citizens Conference on State Legislatures, a tax-exempt research and education organization in St. Louis, whose work was financed by private foundations.*

The CCSL analysis ranked the Texas legislature 38th among the fifty states on the basis of criteria chosen to show how functional, accountable, informed, independent, and representative legislatures were, compared to what the CCSL said the public should expect as mini-

*Director of the study was Larry Margolis, who was a chief staff aide to Jesse Unruh when he was the powerful but reform-minded Democratic speaker of the California Assembly. Unruh's leadership helped produce extensive legislative reforms which may have accounted for the fact that California ranked first in the CCSL comparative study of state legislatures.

mal standards. Texas ranked as the 45th most functional legislature, 36th most accountable, 43rd most informed, 45th most independent, and 17th most representative. Judging by the CCSL criteria, Texas would have ranked even higher in the "representative" category if all of the House members were elected from single-member districts, rather than most from single-member districts and some from multi-member districts. Also, other than Texas only Massachusetts and New Jersey among the major urban-industrial states were placed among the lower twenty-five states in the over-all rank-ordering of legislative capacity for effectiveness.

Analysts for the CCSL study—including members of each legislature—stressed that the study was not designed to measure the quality of a legislative body's work, but rather to gauge to what extent a legislature "has the necessary operational equipment to do its job" and "to act in a responsible, democratic manner." So a Texan reading only that his legislature ranked 38th nationally might have been misled—he might have blamed his elected officials exclusively when he should have blamed himself and his fellow voters as well. For about half of the faults ascribed to the Texas Legislature by the CCSL study were a result of constitutional restraints imposed by a constitution written in 1875. The other faults were directly attributable to legislators who benefited from the way the Legislature did or failed to do its job.

It was easier in the spring of 1971, however, to simply complain about the Legislature in the context of the stock-fraud case. The task was made no less easy later in the year by the September 23, 1971, special report filed by the Travis county grand jury when it indicted Mutscher, Shannon, McGinty, and Osorio:

"It is the opinion of the July session of the Travis county grand jury that some Texas lawmakers, who have been elected by the voters of Texas to these high positions of trust, were too busy granting political favors and being influenced in exchange for 'turning a fast buck' to be concerned about good government for the people. There is dire need of reform so that good laws for the protection and well-being of our citizens might be passed.

"This grand jury was, as far as we know, one of the first groups of individuals to even read the controversial House bills 72 and 73 creating state deposit insurance for banks. These bills were rushed through, and the Texas Banking Commission had not even been consulted or contacted regarding their advantages and disadvantages to the bank depositors of the state. Neither were any of Texas' most knowledgeable and respected bankers consulted about the so-called merits of these bills. This is but one example of the shortcomings of the present Legislature.

"We believe that, beyond the indictments which we have acted upon, there are questionable practices carried on by some of our high state officials. We deplore this fact and would hope that these practices will cease, so that our state may no longer be embarrassed before the nation."

By the end of 1971, apparently, it was even easier for the public to point the finger of responsibility at individual statewide officials and political figures.

The Texas Poll for December 19 revealed that a remarkably high 87 per cent of all registered voters were aware of "the stock scandals in which some Texas government officials have been accused of wrongdoing." Additionally, voters singled out individuals who "acted improperly" with amazing specificity, even without names being suggested by the pollsters. Governor Preston Smith and House Speaker Mutscher, for example, were cited as having acted improperly by an identical 46 per cent of Texas voters aware of the scandal, although Mutscher's bribery indictment had been front-page news in every area of the state and Smith had not been indicted at all. By contrast, Dr. Elmer Baum, the former banking board member and state Democratic chairman who split a $125,000 stock-deal profit with Smith, was named by only 8 per cent of the voters. And Representative Shannon of Fort Worth and speaker's aide McGinty, who were jointly indicted with Mutscher on a charge of conspiracy to accept a bribe, were relegated to the category of "others," with 7 per cent. But Lieutenant Governor Barnes—whose only implication in the scandal was that claimed by a confessed swindler—was named by 21 per cent of the voters aware of the stock-fraud case. And Attorney General Crawford Martin, whose connection with the scandal was that he turned down as too expensive and speculative a Frank Sharp "tip" on NBL stock, was named by 7 per cent as having acted improperly.

By the end of 1971, too, the Texas voting public had been confronted with another scandal of sorts—one involving the conservatively estimated $100 million-a-year coin-operated amusement machine industry and its influence over the legislative process.

The vending industry controversy started, oddly, with the 1969 passage by the Legislature of a so-called "reform" bill. The bill, sponsored by Representative James H. Clark of Dallas in the House and Senator Oscar Mauzy of Dallas in the Senate, grew out of a 1968 between-sessions investigation of the vending industry by the House General Investigating committee. That committee's investigatory data never were revealed, for reasons still unexplained in February, 1972, but its studies demonstrated that coin-amusement machine owners had "muscled" their way into the tavern business by a variety of questionable practices and that the tavern-juke box relationship represented a law enforcement problem. So Clark's bill had two basic goals—to keep vending machine owners out of the tavern business and to prevent the vending industry from monopolizing the juke box, pin-ball machine, and automated pool table business.

But Ed Wendler of Austin, an attorney who was lobbying for the Texas Vending Association, managed to amend the bill in the Senate to satisfy the industry. And during the hectic final hours of the 1969 legislative session, when it appeared that either Wendler's bill or no bill would pass, the measure was approved by Clark, Mauzy and the Legislature. Clark and Mauzy said later they were not aware that Wendler, the vending industry's lobbyist, had amended the bill in such a way that it produced the direct opposite result from what Clark originally intended in two important respects. The bill, as it finally passed under the guiding hand of the very industry it was supposed to reform, tended to strengthen the power of the vending machine owners: although it prohibited vending operators from owning tavern licenses, it permitted them to own the real estate on which taverns were located; and it prohibited tavern operators from owning their own vending machines, but rather forced them to lease machines from vending firms—at a lower tavern operator "take" from the machines, too. (A separate licensing provision also effectively forced restaurant owners to lease vending machines from vending firms.)

This blatant example of lobby influence on the legislative process was supplemented, in a sense, by the 1971 bill that created the Texas Vending Commission. The vending industry by then had changed lobbyists and hired James C. Day of Brookshire, a former House member with all the establishment credentials, including a wife on the State Democratic Executive Committee. Day proposed an industry-backed bill to create the regulatory and fee-collecting vending commission, but with only three members and with all three selected from the vending industry, and further to insulate the large vending firm owners from competition by raising licensing fees. The Legislature did not swallow the whole package. The commission membership was increased to nine, with three representing the industry, three the general public, and three from state government (the attorney general, the Department of Public Safety director, and the consumer credit commissioner). And the license fees were adjusted, although a minimum fee of $50 was required from the owner of just one machine and yet a maximum fee of $3,000 was set for the vending firm with, say, 10,000 machines. Once more, as in the stock-fraud scandal, a bill backed by only a small segment of the public was approved in the final hours of a legislative session.

Governor Smith actually brought the scandal to light when he made his appointments to the Vending Commission in September, 1971. As chairman, Smith chose Raymond B. "RB" Williams of Dallas, who probably was the largest vending firm operator in Texas and who had hired the lobbyists for the Texas Vending Association. Williams had been a key figure in the 1968 vending industry investigation, and at one point went to court in an attempt to keep from testifying and producing his companies' records before the House committee. Williams also contributed $5,000 to Governor Smith's 1970 re-election campaign. Smith's other two industry appointees and two of the so-called public representatives on the commission had business ties to the industry, so a vending operator with problems before the commission could expect a favorable hearing. Even after newspaper investigations had detailed the industry's—and particularly Williams'—role in changing the 1969 "reform" bill and in writing the 1971 commission-creating bill, Smith refused to reconsider his appointments. The House General Investigating Committee, however, resurrected its three-years-dead study of the vending industry and promised to have corrective legislative recommendations in time for the 1973 session.

The legitimate reform movement, meanwhile, gained momentum from the scandals and mini-scandals of the 1969 and 1971 legislative sessions. In addition to literally dozens of reform candidates announcing against incumbent lawmakers who had been close to the lobby-controlled powers of the legislative leadership, local groups of citizens began banding together to seek changes in the way the Legislature was doing its business.

An Austin group called Citizens for a Better Legislature, for example, announced it would seek support for such basic reforms as limiting the House speaker to a single two-year term, raising the pay of lawmakers from $4,800 a year, prohibiting House-Senate conference committees from adding to bills material that had not been approved by either body, and making other improvements in the legislative committee system. The Austin group—headed mostly by retired professional men, several with long backgrounds in state government —said in a statement, "We were disturbed, as are a great many thoughtful Texans, over the seemingly widespread distrust of and lack of confidence in our elected officials, and particularly our lawmakers. This attitude

on the part of the public is understandable, even ines-
capable, in view of the turmoil of the past year." The
statement added, "When the people lose respect for
their government, the foundations of our democratic
system begin to crumble. There can be no respect for
the law unless there is respect for the lawmaker."

Citizens for a Better Legislature specifically criticized
two aspects of the legislative process—"the accretion
of power in the speaker's office . . . [which] tends to
place inordinate power in that office to dominate and
control the action of committees and their leaders" and
the "inadequacy" of the committee system with its
duplication of effort, its erratic and capricious handling
of bills, and its lack of coordination between House
and Senate. In defense of its avoiding direct criticism
of Speaker Mutscher, the CBL added, "We ought to
devote our attention to the shortcomings in the legislative system rather than to the faults of the men
involved in it. We do not seek either to help or hurt
any single individual."

A Fort Worth group took a different and somewhat
more direct approach. Spokesmen for the Citizens Association for Reform said the bipartisan organization
actually would endorse legislative candidates pledged
to a specific reform program. The association's goals
included enactment of a law requiring full public disclosure of campaign contributions and expenditures by
legislative and speakership candidates; creation of a
permanent legislative ethics investigating committee; a
limitation on conference committees' power; and a ban
on seeking pledges for the speakership during a regular
session.

"Because of the stock scandals, all [1972] candidates
will declare they are for reforms in the legislative
process," said Harold Hammett, a lawyer active in the
association. "We want to inform voters how candidates
stand on specific proposals which we regard as necessary to restore public confidence in the legislature."

And, sure enough, many legislators not previously
known as being reform-minded *did* jump on the reform
bandwagon. Even Speaker Mutscher and his Rules committee chairman, Representative Jim Nugent of Kerr-

ville, were converted. Mutscher announced that an unnoticed resolution passed by the House empowered him
to establish a fifteen-member committee to study "all
aspects of improving and facilitating the legislative process." The speaker said that among the subjects for
consideration was a limited seniority system—something he had opposed vehemently for years and something that inherently would reduce the power of the
speaker. Nugent announced that an equally unnoticed
and partially conflicting House resolution designated
the Rules committee as a between-sessions reform
study group. Nugent started his own committee's work
by proposing a series of reforms of his own—several
of which he had voted against a few months earlier
when he was still a faithful Mutscher servant.

There was no mystery about the sudden conversion
of the established powers to the reform program. Reform had been needed for years. During 1971 the need
simply became more dramatic and impelling, both to
those who for years had decried the perversion of the
legislative process for private gain and by those who
had participated in the perversion.

Indeed, it is conceivable that some future successful
reform group will build a monument to a non-drinking,
non-smoking, ecumenical Houston banker and attach a
plaque dedicating it to "Frank Sharp, the man who
made all of this possible."

CHAPTER
THIRTEEN

Where the Future Action Is

There is no simple way to approach reform of the Texas Legislature. It is a task that must take into consideration the fact that 181 elected individuals are paid $4,800 a year to run a state government that costs more than $7 billion every two years to serve the needs of more than 11 million Texans. And the Legislature's job, already massive in terms of volume and complexity, is destined to become more difficult in the years ahead. During the regular session of 1971, the legislators introduced a total of 2,731 bills and passed about one-third of them. That was a 17 per cent increase over the 1969 session's workload, and every index shows that the number of bills introduced will increase in at least the same proportion during the 1973 regular session and beyond.

Insightful politicians—and the pundits who watch them—have observed for at least a decade that the Legislature must be democratized and modernized. But precious little has been done of fundamental significance to making the legislative process in Texas responsive to *all* the people or in persuading a majority of the legislators themselves that it is, indeed, possible to be both independent *and* effective.

Some progress has been made, to be sure. In the last decade alone, legislators have been given private individual offices and a minimal start toward having adequate staff assistance. The Legislative Council, the bill-drafting and research arm of the Legislature, and the Legislative Budget Board, the repository of the Legislature's tax and appropriations expertise, have been upgraded, expanded, and professionalized. Decorum in the House and Senate chambers has been improved, so that a legislator who is interested at least has an *opportunity* to keep up with what is being done.

But progress has been slight, given the magnitude of the problem. As has been true for years, the business lobby still by and large controls the election of the House speaker—in conjunction with key House members whose incumbency is rarely threatened because of their ability to "deliver" on back-home projects and because lobby campaign contributions make an anti-incumbent's race all the less likely to succeed. The same has been true, perhaps with the exception of Preston Smith's election, with the lieutenant governor—the presiding officer of the Senate, whose legislative powers are analogous to those of the speaker, usually is elected by a margin that correlates more or less precisely with the amount of business lobby support he receives. (Most dominant of all the House figures for the last decade has been Bill Heatly of Paducah, chairman of the Appropriations committee. But Heatly's influence deteriorated badly in 1971 because of his involvement in the stock-fraud case and his especially vindictive performance as chairman. There can be no direct parallel to Heatly in the more independent, specialized, and personality-oriented Senate. But Senator Bill Moore of Bryan, the State Affairs committee chairman, comes as close as anyone to being the lobby's power broker in the Senate.)

Similarly, the business lobby, to a discouraging extent, still controls the legislative process—the flow as well as the substance of bills of concern to the special interests. It is not at all unexpected or even out of place for a lobbyist to write a bill, have it referred to a friendly committee, direct the subcommittee's efforts, prepare whatever amendments are necessary, and secure committee approval for the bill. All that the bill sponsor—the House or Senate member who formally introduces the measure but who may know next to nothing about it—has to do is give a brief explanation of it, answer or avoid answering a few questions, and ask for a vote. Essentially the same process, with variations for what lobbyists call "leadership problems," is repeated in the other body.

The 1969 passage of Frank Sharp's bank-deposit insurance bills and, to a lesser extent, the 1969 and 1971 passage of the vending industry bills might demonstrate to the cynical unbeliever that, in the old French phrase, the more things change the more they stay the same. Both situations resulted from the same basic ingredients: over-burdened, under-paid, and voter-wary legislators, eager to go home, were faced in the waning hours of a legislative session with the prospect of passing legislation that was supported only by a small clique of very narrow-interest business hustlers, whose private interests in the bills were couched, characteristically, in terms of the public interest. The bills had not been thoroughly aired in public, either as to the intent of the sponsors or as to the effect of the bills, and no expert testimony was possible because of the time frame within which passage or non-passage had to occur. As a result, most legislators voted blindly, normally following someone else's lead rather than making a decision on their own.

Passage of the Sharpstown bank bills and the vending industry's self-help bills did not, however, reflect unusual circumstances. The bills involved just happened to be rather dramatic examples of poor legislative practice due to the stock-fraud scandal and the later imbroglio over the Texas Vending Commission.

Although talking about Frank Sharp's bills, Lieutenant Governor Barnes could have been talking about any sleazy legislation when he plaintively told the Texas AFL-CIO convention in Dallas on August 13, 1971: "Maybe I should have known there was something wrong with the bills. Maybe the Legislature and the governor should have known. Maybe the press should have known. But the fact is that the only controversy at all in the Senate was on personalities and not on the bills themselves. *There was no controversy in the banking industry and none in the press.*" (emphasis added)

Of course there was no "controversy" in the banking

industry. No representative of the industry had been called to testify, in any form, and bankers had not even been consulted through their trade association. Nor had state banking and insurance officials been consulted, so there was no "controversy" in that corner, either. And as for the press, the Capitol reporters were boxed in by the same pressures of lack of time and information that impinged on the legislators.

Despite all these problems, it must be stressed that another scandal in the Frank Sharp mold *can* be avoided and the legislative process in general *can* be improved. The old political axiom—that if you throw the rascals out, all you get is a new bunch of rascals—is not necessarily true. Because a new group of "rascals," properly guided by an informed and concerned public opinion, can and will make sure that neither they nor anyone else have the *ability* to distort public policy in the style of the Texas Legislature over the last generation or so.

Genuine reform will cost money. It will demand some constitutional and statutory change. It may require the sacrifice of ambition by some extremely talented public servants. And it definitely will take a concerted effort by the citizenry. But whatever the price, it will be a bargain for the voters of Texas in the long range.

What follows here, then, are some reform proposals that should produce meaningful change in and around an assembly that has been notoriously unresponsive to change. The legislative reforms are divided into groups of ideas that would liberate the Legislature generally, reduce the powers of the presiding officers, strengthen the knowledge and decision-making capacity of members, increase the efficiency and cohesion of House-Senate action, and update and expand the lobby regulation laws and practices. Subsequent sections contain proposed changes in the way the executive branch deals with the Legislature and with special-interest groups, plus the all-important area of ethical standards of conduct for public officials.

Many of the ideas presented here have been discussed for years. Some have long been a matter of consensus among reformers, but have been blocked by those in power. The list is neither exhaustive nor exclusive, but rather is designed to stimulate public action toward the end of honest, informed, democratic government that can function effectively without regard to the individuals who may control it at any given time.

* * *

Liberate the Legislature

Certainly we should expect our elected representatives to do their jobs with reasonable speed compatible with the deliberation that the constitution assumes. But the job of state government has become so burdensome and time-consuming that the constitution's restriction of a 140-day regular session of the Legislature every two years is patently ridiculous. Just as private industry would not insist that the board of directors of a $3.5 billion-a-year corporation should complete its work in a series of once-a-month, one-hour meetings, neither should the public require that the Legislature do its $3.5 billion-a-year work in a limited time span. It would be wiser not to have any restriction on the timing or length of a legislative session.

Similarly, a constitutional limitation on legislators' salaries seems outdated and unduly rigid. Salaries of $400 per month—$9,600 for a two-year House term, for instance—written into a century-old constitution would make the original Federalists weep. Salaries of $8,400 per year, approved in an amendment subject to voters' endorsement at the November, 1972, election likewise are too chary. The Citizens Conference on State Legislatures recommended that annual legislative salaries in Texas be set at about $15,000, which may be a little rich for traditionally stingy Texas voters; $12,000 a year probably would be a decent starting place. Whatever the salary level, however, it should not be written into the constitution but rather should be established either by law or by act of an appointed, public-spirited salary commission whose recommendations should be subject to legislative approval.

Rewrite the Constitution

The entire Texas constitution needs to be re-written in the true style of a basic governmental document. What Texas has now is not even as good as an overblown collection of laws; it is a conflicting, confusing, confounding hodge-podge that inordinately complicates the lawmaking process and unnecessarily clogs the courtrooms. If any given 181-member Legislature could agree on a Daniel Webster deal with the devil, it probably would be to get the Texas constitution off their backs, replace it with a real constitution, and leave the lawmaking out of it.

Reduce the Powers of Presiding Officers

In both the House and the Senate, the presiding officer has a disproportionate amount of influence over the legislative process. In the House, the speaker is just one of 150 members elected from prescribed constituencies, but he has made himself far more equal than his 149 colleagues. In the Senate, the lieutenant governor is not even elected as a senator and is, in fact, a member of the executive rather than the legislative branch, yet he has arrogated legislative powers parallel to, if not greater than, those of the speaker. This is not to say that the presiding officers should be stripped of all powers—that they should reign but not rule. It is to say that the very fact of a presiding officer's having too much power destroys, to some extent, the effectiveness of the individual elected legislator. The trend of the 1950's and 1960's was toward more power for the presiding officers and correspondingly less for the members of the House and Senate. That trend needs to be at least stopped, if not reversed.

Since the crucial draftsmanship and questioning of legislation is done by committees, a good way to start would be to inhibit the presiding officer's ability to control committees by stacking them with members friendly to him. Under current practice, a new speaker or lieutenant governor could change committee assignments in such a way that no committee would have a hold-over member from the previous session. A great deal of expertise is lost by the presiding officer's whimsical or designedly political changing of committee assignments. Much more potential expertise is never developed for the same reason. One solution would be a modified senority system in which members who are re-elected to the Legislature retain their old committee assignments as long as they want them. The presiding officer should, however, be able to appoint a committee chairman and vice chairman from among those who served on that committee in the previous session.

Presiding officers should not exercise the power of referring bills to committee, either. That job should be turned over to the Rules committees of the House and Senate, with the fall-back protection that a bill could be referred to another committee by a simple majority vote of the House or Senate. Presiding officers too often abuse the power to refer bills—to hostile committees in the case of bills they do not want passed and to friendly committees for bills they do want passed. Once more, the presiding officer's political sledge-hammer should not be that large.

While they are expanding their roles, the Rules committees also should take over completely the preparation of the so-called "calendars"—the daily agendas of bills to be approved or rejected. Presiding officers, particularly in the House, now tend to involve themselves too deeply in the political shenanigans of bill scheduling. There is a special problem in the Senate, which hardly uses calendars at all because senators pass most bills under a rule that allows quickie passage of bills with the support of two-thirds of the Senate.

The Rules committees should be required to put bills on the calendars in the order in which the bills were reported out of committee, so that members of the Rules panel could not delay or completely prohibit action on bills approved by legislative committees. This happens frequently in the House, in blatant disregard for a bill sponsor's right to have the House vote on his bill.

As the stock-fraud case showed, hurry-up passage of bills produced a euphoria of action that belied a lack of deliberation. Bills approved out of committee should not appear on any daily agenda until 48 hours later, with perhaps a 24-hour delay during special sessions. And the agenda for each working day should be available to members at least 24 hours in advance—48 hours in the case of so-called local and consent bills, measures that either do not have statewide application or are not being contested.

In another step to equalize the power of the presiding officer *vis a vis* the other legislators, the Administration committees of the House and Senate should handle all personnel matters, subject to vote by the members. The presiding officers should have no hiring or firing power except over their own staffs, just like the other legislators. And each body should maintain an up-to-date monthly listing of all legislative employees' salaries—including the Legislative Council and Legislative Budget Board staffs—and all committee expenses, both during the session and in the interim.

Finally, the Senate should start using an electronic vote-recording device such as that in the House, not solely because it is a time-saving machine but also because it provides an instantaneous and remarkably accurate vote record. Both voting machines then should be adjusted so that the lights—green for yes, red for no, white for not voting—do not come on until the vote has been completed. This would destroy the follow-the-leader syndrome that many legislators adopt out of stupidity, cupidity, or laziness. Visitors to the Legislature often are shocked to see grown men standing up in the front of the chambers, waving either one finger (for yes) or two fingers (for no) in the air to tell their unenlightened friends how they should vote. It is a corruptive habit that would be minimized by not allowing the sheep to see how others have voted before casting their own votes.

TEXAS UNDER A CLOUD

*Strengthen the Knowledge and Decision-making
Capacity of Members*

One of the most basic problems a legislator faces is
that he is expected to do too much with the limited
resources and time at his disposal. He does not have
enough secretarial help, if he is from an urban area,
to keep up with his mail. He does not have enough
legal assistance to keep up with the volume of bills
that must be analyzed—much less the long-range prob-
lem-solving and research help he needs to avoid being
only a responder to crises. His committee work is not
necessarily too heavy, but it is too spread out and thus
cannot be thorough if he has say, five or six committee
assignments, and sometimes is expected to be at more
than one committee meeting at the same time. So the
legislator needs more personnel on his own staff, both
during the sessions and even when the Legislature is
not in session. (The Senate has made great strides in
this area in the last few years, but the House has not).

The committee structure of the entire Legislature
should be modified, both to cut down on the number
of committees and to increase the competence of the
committees. There need not be more than, say, 15 to
20 committees, and the jurisdictions of House and Senate committees should be coterminous, to avoid the
duplication and confusion that, sometimes intention-
ally, result in poor legislation. And committees should
be given permanent, year-around professional staff
aides—a minimum of one lawyer and a clerk for each
committee and extra staff members for the major committees. Legislators should be limited in the number of
committees to which they are assigned—no more than
two committee assignments in the House, for example,
and no more than three in the Senate. In the cases of
heavy-workload committees, at least, chairmen of the
panels on rules, taxes, appropriations, and state affairs
should not serve as chairmen of any other committees.

Because it already is difficult enough for legislators
to keep up with what goes on daily, all subcommittee,
committee, and legislative sessions should be tape-re-

corded, with the recordings available at all times, day or night, for legislators' or their aides' use. Some standard should be set for the determination of whether written transcripts of the recordings are made—to permit 50 representatives or 10 senators, for example, to demand a written record of what happened on a particular bill on a particular day.

Both the House and the Senate should prohibit the practice known as "floor-reporting" bills, in which committees meet hurriedly on the floor of the chamber, while other legislative business is being transacted, and approve bills without hearings and usually without opportunity to even read the bills being considered. In this same connection, both houses ought to have non-suspendable rules requiring 48 hours' public notice that a given bill is to be heard by a committee or subcommittee. There probably are not more than two or three bills every two years whose passage is so urgent that floor-reporting can be justified—and it is important to remember that Frank Sharp's bank-deposit insurance bills were approved in the Senate by this very mechanism, which could be called blind voting.

Perhaps the most significant mechanical change that both houses should make is to move toward the Congressional system on committee reports, the documents that accompany bills and that are supposed to detail every aspect of the bills. No bill or conference committee report should be accepted for action by the House or Senate unless it contains (1) an official comptroller's estimate of the cost or revenue impact of the bill for the next two or four years; (2) a statement of position on the bill by every state agency the bill affects; and (3) an attorney general's statement on the constitutional and legal impact of the legislation, on both state and local governments. This would make it less likely for the Legislature to pass the author's explanation of the bill rather than the substance of the bill itself.

There are a number of other things that can be done to improve the legislators' ability to understand what he is voting on: bills should not be finally passed until all amendments have been incorporated into the text; proxy voting should be prohibited in all subcommittee and committee meetings, because an absent legislator has no business taking part in a decision of any kind; no substantive policy "riders," which are extraneous orders to state agencies, should be permitted; neither house should be able to consider its own bills in the last week of a regular session, to prevent the bill-a-minute pace of bad legislation in the waning and unwatchful hours; and the politically potent agendas full of members' local and uncontested bills should be prohibited in the last week of the session.

Generally, then, the idea should be to slow down the legislative process, increase the individual member's chance of understanding what he is doing, and professionalize the handling of legislation in committees.

Improve Efficiency and Cohesion
Of House-Senate Action

One of the major developments of the 1970's should be to make the House and Senate work more rationally and effectively together. There now is little question about the need to limit the power of ten-member House-Senate conference committees, for example; the only real issue is precisely how to do it. Conferees should be limited to adjusting the differences between House and Senate versions of the same bill. They should have no power to add material not included in either version, they should not be able to eliminate material that is not in dispute, and they should be required to compromise between the lowest and the highest figures (in the cases of taxes and appropriations) or below the high figures if only one bill deals with a given subject. Conference committees also should be forced to give public notice of their meetings, and the meetings should be open to the public. One way to make these requirements effective—and to make other rules effective, too—would be to permit an automatic and fatal point of order against any committee report that does not comply fully with the rules.

That would send an errant committee or conference committee back to the drawing board.

While the House and Senate are drawing up joint rules, which should be in effect from session to session and subject to change only by a joint resolution, they should establish uniform rules on committee procedure and establish in detail the parallel jurisdictions of House and Senate committees. And to avoid the kind of impasse where no bill is passed, one body should be prohibited from passing a bill on any subject covered by a bill that the other body has passed previously. Too, if the House State Affairs committee is considering an abortion law repeal bill, for example, a Senate-passed bill on the same subject should be required to go to the State Affairs committee, rather than somewhere else.

And the joint rules should prohibit the consideration of a conference committee report by either House or Senate until the report has been available to the entire legislature for at least three days—five days in the cases of appropriations and tax bills. Conference committee reports often are so complex that members do not have time to find out quickly how the differences between House and Senate bills were compromised.

Update and Expand Lobby Regulation

Contrary to popular impressions, lobbyists are not inherently evil. They have a constitutional right, just as any individual citizen does, to express opinions about legislation and, yes, even to protect their clients' interests. But because they are neither totally benign nor totally malignant, lobbyists need extensive regulation, because of their wide, deep ,and pervasive influence over the legislative process. Again contrary to what might be a popular impression, by and large lobbyists do not earn their livelihoods by making big pay-offs to get bills passed or killed. Most successful lobbyists make their influence felt by two means— campaign contributions a year before a legislative session and sheer proximity of technical and legal expertise during a session. The latter is an entirely legitimate—and even a valuable—function that should not and probably cannot be curtailed.

But a lobby's campaign contributions are another matter, and one not currently subject to effective regulation. Lobbyists are required to report publicly only those expenditures made during a legislative session for "direct communication" with legislators—a term narrowly but imprecisely defined in the law. The "direct communication" loophole essentially prohibits the public from knowing which special interests spent how much to influence whom. Minimally, then, lobbyists should be required to report quarterly between sessions, and monthly during sessions, *all* expenditures and campaign contributions made in efforts to influence either the election of candidates or the flow of legislation, as well as expenditures to create good will with candidates or incumbent legislators. (And it should be a crime for a special interest not to report a change in lobbyists within a week of the time the change is made.) The publicly-reported information should be broken down into detail by client, if the lobbyist has more than one, so that a lobbyist cannot merely list all of his clients, all of his expenditures, and all of his campaign contributions without specifying whose money was spent for what purpose.

Conceptually, another fundamental change needs to be made as to who is required to register as a lobbyist. Current law recognizes a distinction between a person lobbying in his own interest and a person lobbying in behalf of others, so that self-interest lobbyists are not required to register. Admittedly, it would create a slight book-keeping problem, but all persons lobbying on any kind of legislation—whether for the Texas Manufacturers Association or for the Texas AFL-CIO—should be registered. This self-interest loophole was used by Waggoner Carr, a bank director, and John Osorio, an insurance company stock-holder and bank director, as an excuse for not registering as lobbyists on the Sharpstown bank bills.

There is an additional problem of protocol involving lobbyists who are former House and Senate members, because as former members they are entitled to the so-called "privileges of the floor"—which means they can walk around the House and Senate chambers, chatting with old friends and making new friends. Although they are not supposed to do so, they frequently do a little lobbying while they are walking around— and they should be prohibited from exercising their floor privileges if they are lobbyists in any sense of the word. Legislative courtesy should not be extended to permit the abuse of prerogatives dating from prior service. Another touchy problem is that legislative employees, including aides to the presiding officers, often "work the floor" (a euphemism for lobbying) in violation of existing rules—and sometimes in tandem with paid, professional lobbyists.

Finally, since this is a hazy area in terms of law enforcement, the attorney general should be given specific and detailed responsibility for enforcing the lobby registration and reporting laws. The House and Senate have proved themselves incapable of policing their own shops.

Executive Branch

The governor of Texas, whoever he is at any given moment, is at a distinct disadvantage in dealing with the Legislature. For while he has the right to recommend courses of public policy action to the lawmakers, he really has only the power of the veto to make his points stick. If he uses the veto power extensively, he jeopardizes his own executive and administrative powers—because the Legislature has the power to control the governor's office appropriations. Yet in considering his use of the veto, the governor is woefully short of assistance to analyze legislation over which he alone has final power of approval or disapproval. Thus, the governor needs more staff assistants, at least during and shortly after a legislative session, to do nothing but analyze bills, particularly in the context of what individuals or special-interest groups pressed for passage of

TEXAS UNDER A CLOUD

the bills, who opposed them and why, and what the bills actually would do (as opposed to what the bill sponsors *said* they would do).

State agencies likewise need more personnel for the analysis of legislation, particularly if the Legislature adopts a rule requiring that each piece of legislation approved by a committee or conference committee be accompanied by an "impact" statement from each affected state agency. This need for staff assistance will be unusually acute in the attorney general's office. But if the attorney general's office were more involved in the objective—not political—analysis of pending legislation, the state would not be spending as much money defending itself in court on obviously unconstitutional legislation. Other state agencies also should be given, at least during and immediately after legislative sessions, the power to hire lawyers with no other responsibilities than to study legislation affecting the agencies. (The lawyers should be hired *by* the agencies but with the approval of the attorney general's office, which should be concerned only with the attorney's competence).

The state agencies also should be forced, by the attorney general, to apply the law that requires visitors to the agency to sign a log of appearances. But the law should be expanded to require that the log reflect the purpose of the visitor's appearance, the name of the agency official visited, and an acknowledgement of the visitor's statement by the official himself. This would complicate somewhat the current procedure, which some state agencies only began enforcing when the stock-fraud case broke in 1971. But it is important to realize that many state agency policy decisions are affected by these private "visits"—which are made by lobbyists and legislators as well as private citizens.

Ethical Standards of Conduct for Public Officials

With Attorney General Martin's January 6, 1972, opinion that the Legislature's 1971 last-minute ethics law was unconstitutional, the state's ethical standards for selected public officials reverted to the 1957 law that was passed in the wake of an earlier legislative scandal. The 1957 law is inherently weak in that its main prohibition is against business or professional interests or obligations that are "in substantial conflict" with the public servant's official duties. Certainly we should be able to expect, as voters and taxpayers, that public officials have no conflict of interest problems and that they reveal enough of their personal finances to indicate whether those problems exist. Specifically, all top state officials—elected or appointed, paid or unpaid—who make or direct the implementation of public policy should be required to file sworn public financial disclosure statements detailing assets and liabilities and net worth based on market value. Local government officials need not be included, as local entities can set their own standards; and state officials below the level of agency executive directors need not be included. But surely, even beyond the distrust and suspicion of public officials and their private lives that were generated by the stock-fraud case, we can expect the Legislature to respond with a rationally designed, legal financial disclosure law that will permit the people to decide for themselves whether their public servants are subject to or guilty of conflicts of interest.

Beyond that disclosure, too, we should establish some other standards. No state official should be allowed to earn income from or own an interest in any business entity that is regulated in any way by any state agency (other than by payment of taxes); current law applies a lesser prohibition against an official's relationship with a business entity regulated by his own state agency. Further, there should be an absolute prohibition against the lucrative practice of a legislator's appearing for pay, or in his own self-interest, before a state agency (obviously excepting the courts), because the power implicit in serving in the Legislature is sufficient unto itself without the additional impact of practicing before a state agency whose appropriations and duties are controlled by the Legislature. In the case of lawyer-legislators, their law partners or associates also should not be allowed to practice before state agencies, if only because of the sheer invidious discrimination involved in a business association with a legislator. Also, state agencies should be prohibited from offering special favors to state officials, particularly legislators, other than as provided for in the appropriations bill or in published, publicly approved agency records. All state officials should be proscribed from sponsoring, initiating, or participating in (voting, in the case of a legislator) any proposal or decision that directly affects his own financial situation—thus eliminating the exemption for an individual's taking part if it does not help him financially any more than it does others "similarly situated," because the fact is that no one is "similarly situated" to a state official. For legislators, it should be an unethical act, subject to censure and/or removal from office, to sponsor legislation without specifying in writing before the House and Senate who wrote a particular piece of legislation and what individuals, groups, or interests contributed to its creation. Similarly, the governor's office should be required to keep records of contacts about legislation—if for no reason other than to make public what individuals or interests ask that specific legislation be included or not included in the governor's legislative proposals or in the governor's "call" for a special session. (It should be remembered that Governor Preston Smith could not recall, even by February, 1972, who asked him to include Frank Sharp's bank-deposit insurance bills in the 1969 special session call; his memory had to be jogged for him to recall that the bankers association president and former Governor Allan Shivers, also a banker, asked Smith to veto the Sharpstown bank bills). Also, the questionable practice of the so-called "legislative continuance"—permitting a lawyer-legislator to request an automatic trial delay until after a legislative session—should be reformed; perhaps the judge should be given back the power to decide whether the trial should be delayed.

The public also should demand that the existing law on campaign financing disclosure be enforced, using the guidelines announced in December, 1971, by Secretary of State Bob Bullock. Bullock's rules—which would put teeth into the law for the first time in its ignoble and ignored history—should be written into law word for word. In addition, the rules should be extended to apply to political parties, and all campaign financing disclosure reports—by candidates and parties—should be open to the public. The reports should be required every three months, year-round, even in non-election years, and special extra reports should be required 15 days after primary, special, and general elections.

Finally, the Legislature should pass a law eliminating the legal distinction between the disclosure of the name of the owner of record and the name of the beneficial owner. The distinction should not exist, and both the owner of record and the beneficial owner should be recorded on everything that is a matter of public record, subject to criminal penalties for violation. This step would require a great deal of work, admittedly, but it is of obvious and highly significant ethical import. For recognition of the distinction between the owner of record and the beneficial owner, currently embodied explicitly or by implication in a number of Texas laws, leads to the "set-aside," "cover-up," and "designated" ownership mechanisms that are widely used in political circles. Permitting the distinction, and not requiring the disclosure of both owners, allows the individuals involved to lie to the public and makes discovery of conflicts of interest almost impossible.

* * *

Given a set of proposed reforms, as well as the stock-fraud case as an impetus to action, where does the reform movement go and where does its momentum come from? The answer is, to and from the people.

Writing in the December, 1971, issue of *Fortune* magazine, A. James Reichley had these comments about the aftermath of the stock-fraud case:

"Whatever bitter fruits [Frank] Sharp's dreams have borne for his allies and collaborators, their paradoxical effects for Texas may be a better political future. Which of the state's political configurations will capture the spirit of reform is not yet certain. Texas Republicans can argue convincingly that corruption has resulted at least in part from the Democrats' monopoly on power... The liberal Democrats, Texas' other major political out-group, have natural claims on the banner of reform... Actually, the political leaders with the best opportunity to act as agents of reform are the more progressive and adaptable figures among the conservative Democrats ... There is no particular reason why social or fiscal conservatives cannot bring about political reform, as indeed they have in many states that were industrialized before Texas ...

"Much will depend on the attitude of the leaders of the Texas business establishment, who have fueled the campaigns of the conservative Democrats and hold ultimate authority over the business lobbyists in Austin. Up until now, Texas business in general has felt that weak and ineffective state government served its economic interests. In order to preserve its privileges and power, it has been willing to tolerate an occasional Frank Sharp. If the establishment leaders continue in this view, they can still steer the Democratic organization away from reform, and back into the arms of men like [John] Osorio and [Waggoner] Carr. But the result might well be that the voters would at last turn the conservative Democrats out of office—and business would find itself, for the first time in many years, on the outside politically in Texas."

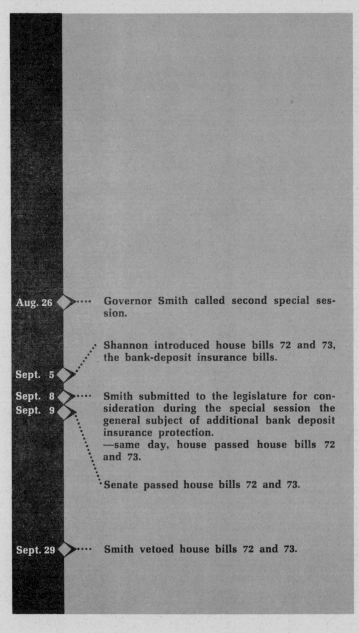

Aug. 26 ····· Governor Smith called second special session.

Shannon introduced house bills 72 and 73, the bank-deposit insurance bills.

Sept. 5

Sept. 8 ····· Smith submitted to the legislature for consideration during the special session the general subject of additional bank deposit insurance protection.

Sept. 9 —same day, house passed house bills 72 and 73.

Senate passed house bills 72 and 73.

Sept. 29 ····· Smith vetoed house bills 72 and 73.